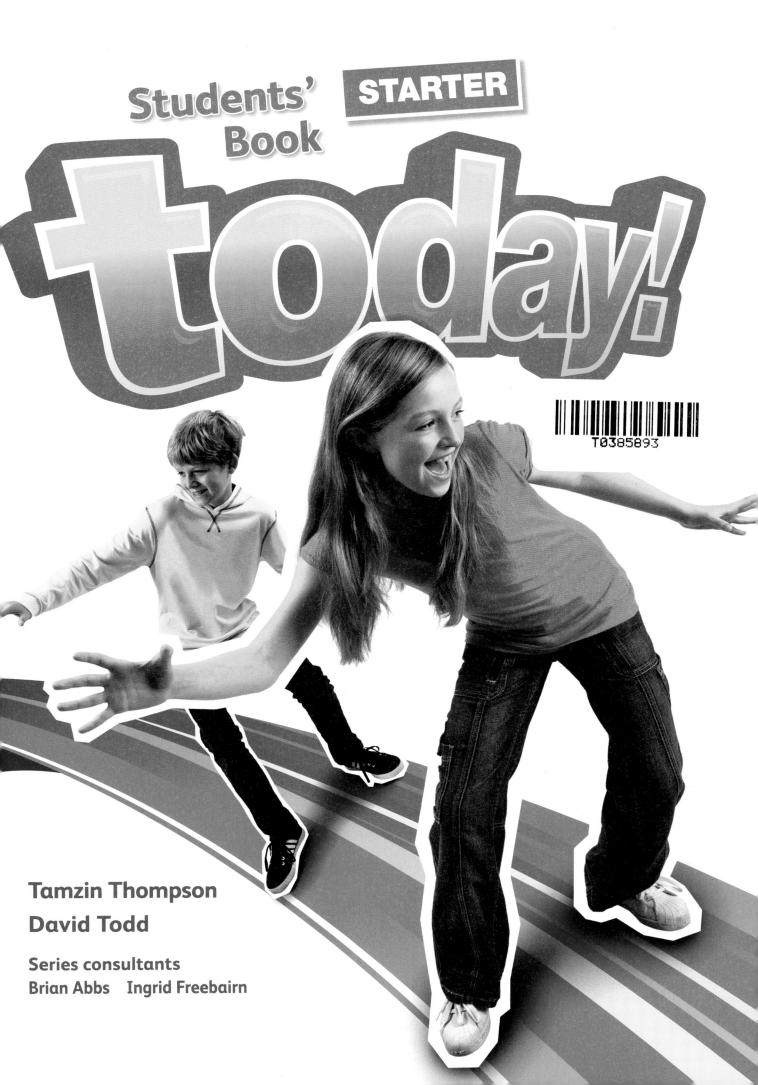

Students' Book

STARTER

today!

T0385893

Tamzin Thompson

David Todd

Series consultants

Brian Abbs   Ingrid Freebairn

Contents

1 Hello.

A I'm Lily.

Lesson aims:
- introduce yourself
- ask someone's name
- spell your name

Presentation

1 (1 02) **Listen and read.**

Lily:	Hello. I'm Lily. What's your name?
Asha:	My name's Asha.
Robbie:	And I'm Robbie.
Asha:	Hi, Robbie.
Raj:	Hello. I'm Raj.
Mrs Patel:	Asha! Raj! Lunch!
Asha:	OK, Mum! Bye, Lily. Bye, Robbie.
Lily/Robbie:	Goodbye, Asha. Goodbye, Raj!

2 (1 03) **Listen and repeat the dialogue.**

English today

- Hello.
- Hi.
- OK.
- Bye.
- Goodbye.

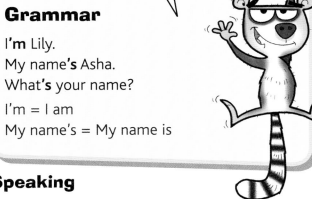

Hi! I'm Lenny!

Grammar

I**'m** Lily.
My name**'s** Asha.
What**'s** your name?

I'm = I am
My name's = My name is

Speaking

3 Say *Hello* to your partner.

A: *Hello.*
B: *Hi.*
A: *I'm ... . What's your name?*
B: *My name's ...*

4 You are a famous sportsperson. Say *Hi* or *Hello* to your partner.

A: *Hi, I'm David. What's your name?*
B: *Hello, David. My name's Serena.*

1 David Beckham

2 Serena Williams

3 Victoria Pendleton

4 Kobe Bryant

Vocabulary: The alphabet

5 1 04 Listen and repeat. Then say the alphabet backwards.

Aa Bb Cc Dd
Ee Ff Gg Hh
Ii Jj Kk Ll Mm
Nn Oo Pp Qq
Rr Ss Tt Uu
Vv Ww Xx
Yy Zz

Listening

6 1 05 Listen and complete the names.

1 L _i_ _l_ y
2 R _____ b _____ _____
3 _____ a _____
4 A _____ _____ a
5 _____ a _____ i _____

About you

7 Say *Hello* to your partner and spell your name.

Hello. I'm Marta Nowak.
M – A – R – T – A   N – O – W – A – K

> Now turn to Unit 1A in the Activity Book. Start on page 1.

B He's my brother.

Presentation

1 🔊 1/06 **Listen and read.**

Robbie:	Hi, Alex. Alex is my little brother.
Raj:	Hi, Alex.
Alex:	Hello.
Raj:	And who's he in the photo?
Robbie:	He's my dad.
Raj:	What's his name?
Robbie:	His name's Eric.
Raj:	And who's she?
Robbie:	She's my mum. Her name's Sally.
Raj:	And that's you and Lily! Nice photo!

2 🔊 1/07 **Listen and repeat the dialogue.**

Vocabulary: Family members

3 🔊 1/08 **Listen and repeat.**

father (dad)   mother (mum)
brother   sister   uncle   aunt   cousin
grandfather (grandad)
grandmother (grandma)

4 **Look at the Baker family tree and write the family members.**

The Baker family

Jerry ¹ *grandfather*

Janice ²

Eric ³

Sally ⁴

Peter ⁵

Patricia ⁶

Lily ⁷

Alex ⁹

Jake ¹⁰

Robbie ⁸

Grammar

Who's he?
He's my dad.
Who's she?
She's my mum.

He's = He is   She's = She is

Speaking

5 **A: You are Raj. B: You are Robbie. Ask and answer about the Baker family in Exercise 4.**

A: *Who's he?*
B: *He's my grandad.*
A: *Who's she?*
B: *She's ...*

6 **Look at the Patel family. You are Asha. Write *He's* or *She's*.**

Asha

1 Deepa

2 Raj

3 Sanjay

4 Devina

1 *She's*........ my mum.
2 .... my brother.
3 .... my dad.
4 .... my grandma.

Grammar

He's my dad.
What's **his** name?
His name's Eric.

She's my mum.
What's **her** name?
Her name's Sally.

7 **Look at the Patel family in Exercise 6 again. Ask and answer.**

1 A: What's her name?
   B: Her name's Deepa.

8 **Choose the correct words. Ask and answer.**

Miley Cyrus: singer and actress

1 A: What's *his / her* name?
   B: *His / Her* name's Miley.

Daniel Radcliffe: actor

2 A: What's *his / her* name?
   B: *His / Her* name's Daniel.

About you

9 **Draw your family tree. Look at the family tree in Exercise 4 to help you. Ask and answer.**

A: *Who's he?*
B: *He's my brother.*
A: *What's his name?*
B: *His name's Felipe.*

> Now turn to Unit 1B in the Activity Book. Start on page 5.

C How old are you?

Lesson aims:
- ask someone's age
- say the days of the week
- count to 50

Presentation

1 **Listen and read.**

Robbie:	It's my birthday today.
Raj:	Really? Happy birthday! How old are you?
Robbie:	I'm eleven. How old are you?
Raj:	I'm ten but I'm eleven on Wednesday.
Robbie:	Cool!
Raj:	Hi, Lily! Wow! What a big present!
Lily:	Yes, it's for my dog. It's his birthday on Thursday.
Raj:	How old is he?
Lily:	He's five.
Robbie:	Oh no! It's a present for Spot, not for me!

2 **Listen and repeat the dialogue.**

English today

- Really?
- Happy birthday!
- Cool!
- Wow!
- What a (big present)!
- Oh no!

Vocabulary: Days of the week

3 **Listen and repeat.**

- Monday
- Tuesday
- Wednesday
- Thursday
- Friday
- Saturday
- Sunday

4 **Cover Exercise 3. Complete the days of the week.**

- [ ] S_t_r_a____
- [ ] __u__s__a__
- [ ] S__n__a____
- [ ] __r__d__y
- [ ] W__d__e__d__y
- [1] M o n d a y
- [ ] T__u__s__a____

5 **Number the days in Exercise 4 in order.**

Grammar

It's my birthday today.
What day **is** it today?

It's = It is

Speaking

6 Look at the planner in Exercise 3.
Point to a day and ask and answer.

A: *What day is it today?*
B: *It's Monday.*

Vocabulary: Numbers 0–50

7 **1 12** Listen and repeat.

0 zero   1 one   2 two
3 three   4 four   5 five
6 six   7 seven   8 eight
9 nine   10 ten   11 eleven
12 twelve   13 thirteen
14 fourteen   15 fifteen
16 sixteen   17 seventeen
18 eighteen   19 nineteen
20 twenty   21 twenty-one
22 twenty-two   23 twenty-three
30 thirty   31 thirty-one
40 forty   50 fifty

Grammar

How old **are** you?   I**'m** eleven.
How old **is** he/she?   He**'s**/She**'s** eleven.
How old **am** I?   You**'re** eleven.

8 **1 13** Complete the questions and answers. Then listen and check.

1 *How* old is Maria?   2 .... is Jack?
  She's eleven.   ....

3 .... you?   4 ....
  ....   your mother?
                                     ....

Writing

9 Write about you and two people in your family.

Hi! My name's Rafal.
I'm ten. My brother is
Danek. He's twelve. He's
cool. She's my mum. Her
name's Magda. She's
thirty-five. She's nice.

> Now turn to Unit 1C in the Activity Book. Start on page 9.

D Revision

1 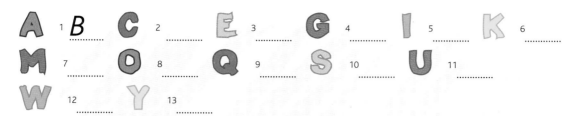 **Complete the letters of the alphabet. Then listen and say the next letter.**

A ¹ *B*   C ²____   E ³____   G ⁴____   I ⁵____   K ⁶____

M ⁷____   O ⁸____   Q ⁹____   S ¹⁰____   U ¹¹____

W ¹²____   Y ¹³____

2 **Look at Ben's family tree. Complete the sentences.**

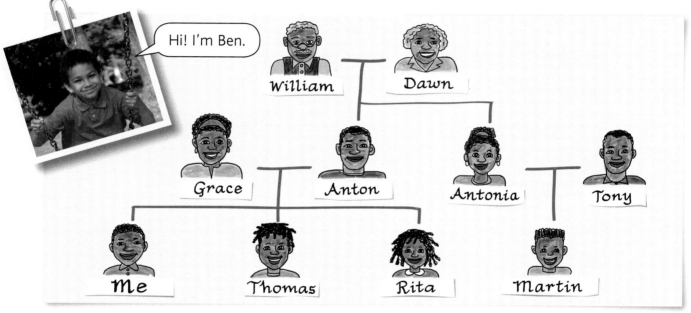

Hi! I'm Ben.

William   Dawn

Grace   Anton   Antonia   Tony

Me   Thomas   Rita   Martin

1 Rita is my _sister_____.
2 Anton is my _____.
3 Thomas is my _____.
4 Antonia is my _____.
5 Dawn is my _____.

6 Martin is my _____.
7 Grace is my _____.
8 Tony is my _____.
9 William is my _____.

3 **Complete the dialogues about Ben's family. Ask and answer.**

1 **A:** Who's she?
  B: ¹ _She's___ my sister.
  A: What's ² _____ name?
  B: ³ _____ name's Rita.
2 **A:** Who's he?
  B: ⁴ _____ my uncle.
  A: What's ⁵ _____ name?
  B: ⁶ _____ name's Tony.

4 **Write the missing numbers in the sequence.**

1 ten, nine, _eight_____, seven
2 two, four, six, _____
3 twenty, nineteen, eighteen, _____
4 twenty, thirty, forty, _____
5 fifty, forty, thirty, _____, ten
6 five, ten, _____, twenty
7 two, four, eight, sixteen _____

5 **Read and choose the correct words. Then act out the dialogue.**

Scott: Hello. ¹(My)/ I'm name's Scott. She's ² my / her sister, Jenny. What's ³ you're / your name?

Amy: ⁴ My / I'm Amy. How old ⁵ is / are you?

Scott: ⁶ I'm / My ten.

Amy: How old ⁷ is / are your sister?

Scott: ⁸ She's / He's twelve.

6 **Unscramble the words. Then complete the questions and answers.**

1 What day is it today?
It's _Saturday_____. (dutaryaS)

2 What day _____ it today?
It's _____. (haryTdus)

3 What _____ today?
It's _____. (saTeyud)

4 What _____?
It's _____. (riyFad)

5 _____?
It's _____. (nyodMa)

6 _____?
_____. (yendsWade)

7 **Look at the dialogues in Exercise 6. Ask and answer.**

A: *What day is it today?*

B: *It's Saturday.*

Song: My family

8 (1/15) **Listen and complete. Then listen and sing.**

He's my ¹ _father_____.
His name's Sam.
She's my ² _____.
Her name's Pam.
He's my ³ _____.
His name's Joe.
She's my ⁴ _____.
Her name's Flo.
He's my ⁵ _____.
His name's Boo.
My ⁶ _____'s Dan.
Who are you?

Pronunciation: /h/

9 (1/16) **Listen and repeat.**

Hi! He's **H**enry! **H**is **h**at is blue.
Henry's ten. **H**ow old are you?

My progress

10 **Read and tick (✓).**

I can:	
introduce myself. *Hello. I'm Lily.*	☐
ask someone's name. *What's your name?*	☐
spell my name. *I'm Marta. M – A – R – T – A.*	☐
talk about my family. *He's my dad.*	☐
ask someone's age. *How old are you?*	☐
say the days of the week. *Monday, Tuesday …*	☐
count to 50. *one, two, three …*	☐

> Turn to Unit 1 Check in the Activity Book on page 13.

pick and mix

Guess what?

NUMBERS AND LETTERS

The letters A, F, H, K, N, Y and Z are all three lines.

The letters A, H, I, M, O, T, U, V, W, X and Y are the same in a mirror. Now you try!

JUST JOKING!

THE 1 2 3 ALPHABET 4 5 6 7 8 9 10 11

There are eleven letters in the alphabet.

Really?

It's true! Look!

Ha ha!

How to ...
make a really cool birthday card!

You need:
- 2 pieces of paper
- glue
- a pair of scissors
- crayons or pens

Step 1: Fold

Step 2: Draw

Step 3: Cut

Step 4: Glue

Step 5: Colour

Step 6: Write

Fun Time!

ALPHABET SOUP

Write the missing letters of the alphabet in the box.
Then order the letters and complete the sentence.

MISSING LETTERS

A

My favourite day is __ __ __ __ __ __ __ __ .

STAR SPOT

Choose the correct words.

Justin Bieber

Justin Bieber [1] *is* / *are* a singer.
[2] *He's* / *She's* from Canada. [3] *His* / *Her* pet is a dog. His name's Sam.

Malia Obama

Malia Obama is from the USA. [4] *His* / *Her* dad [5] *is* / *are* Barack Obama. [6] *His* / *Her* pet is Bo. He's a dog.

JUST JOKING!

What's half of 8?

3! Haha!

2 Favourite things

A It's a book.

Lesson aims:
- ask and answer about possessions
- talk about colours

Presentation

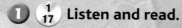 **Listen and read.**

Lily:	Grandad! Look! Number 1 – what's that?
Alex:	I know! It's a ...
Lily:	Sssh, Alex!
Grandad:	It's a book!
Lily:	That's right! And what colour is it, Alex?
Alex:	It's red.
Lily:	OK, Grandad. What's that?
Grandad:	Er ...
Alex:	I know! It's an ice cream! Cool!
Lily:	That's right, Alex!
Grandad:	Well done!

2 **Listen and repeat the dialogue.**

English today
- I know!
- That's right!
- Well done!

Vocabulary: Possessions (1)

3 Listen and repeat. Then match.

> apple bike book camera computer
> football ice cream skateboard TV
> umbrella

1 *skateboard*

1

2

3

4

5

6

7

8

9

10

Grammar

What's that?
It's **a b**ook.
What's that?
It's **an i**ce cream.

4 Look at the pictures in Exercise 3.
Point, ask and answer.

1 **A:** What's that?
 B: It's a skateboard.

Vocabulary: Colours

5 Listen and repeat. Then match.

> black blue brown green grey
> orange pink purple red white
> yellow

1 *black*

Grammar

What colour is it?
It's red/orange.

Speaking

6 Look at the pictures in Exercise 3. Point,
ask and answer.

1 **A:** What's that?
 B: *It's a skateboard.*
 A: *What colour is it?*
 B: *It's purple.*
 A: *That's right!*

About you

7 Choose your favourite possession. Draw
it. Then write about it.

My favourite
possession is my
bike. It's blue.

> Now turn to Unit 2A in the Activity Book. Start on page 14.

B Is it a school book?

Lesson aim:
• ask and answer about everyday objects

Presentation

1 **Listen and read.**

Mum: Robbie! It's late! Here's your bag.
Robbie: Great. Thanks, Mum.
Mum: What's that? Is it a school book?
Robbie: No, it isn't. It's your dictionary.
Mum: Oh. And what's that? Is it my favourite pen?
Robbie: Yes, it is. Sorry!
Mum: That's OK. Hurry up, Robbie!
Robbie: OK, I'm ready now!
Mum: Let's go!

2 **Listen and repeat the dialogue.**

English today

- It's late!
- Here's your (bag).
- Great.
- Thanks.
- Sorry!
- That's OK.
- Hurry up!
- I'm ready now.
- Let's go!

Vocabulary: Everyday objects

3 **Listen and repeat. Then label the picture.**

| bag comic dictionary eraser jacket mobile phone |
| notebook pen pencil case ruler |

1 *mobile phone*

2 ....

3 ....

4 ....

5 ....

6 ....

7 ....

8 ....

9 ....

10 ....

Grammar

Is it a pen?
Yes, it **is**.
Is it a pencil?
No, it **isn't**.

Listening

4 (1 24) **Listen and tick (✓) the correct picture.**

1

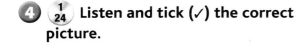

A ✓   B ☐

2

A ☐   B ☐

3

A ☐   B ☐

4

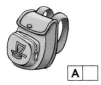 

A ☐   B ☐

Speaking

5 **Look at the picture in Exercise 3. Ask and answer.**

1 A: *What's number one? Is it a pen?*
   B: *No, it isn't. It's a mobile phone.*

1 pen
2 dictionary
3 bag
4 ruler
5 eraser
6 pencil case
7 comic
8 notebook
9 jacket
10 mobile phone

Writing

6 **Write the questions and answers. Ask and answer with your partner.**

1 notebook
   Is it a notebook?
   No, it isn't. It's a dictionary.

2 pencil case
   ....?
   ....

3 pencil
   ....?
   ....

4 eraser
   ....?
   ....

5 ruler
   ....?
   ....

6 bag
   ....?
   ....

7 notebook
   ....?
   ....

8 jacket
   ....?
   ....

Game

7 **A: Choose an object from Exercise 4 or 6. B: Ask questions. Guess the object.**

A: *I'm ready now!*
B: *OK. Is it red?*
A: *No, it isn't.*
B: *Is it black?*
A: *Yes, it is.*
B: *Is it a dictionary?*
A: *Yes, it is.*

> Now turn to Unit 2B in the Activity Book. Start on page 18.

Communication

Speaking: Greetings and personal information

1 **Listen and read.**

Raj is at the sports centre. He's a new member of the basketball club.

1

Raj:	Good morning. I'm here for the basketball club.
Woman:	OK. What's your name?
Raj:	It's Raj Patel.
Woman:	How do you spell 'Patel'?
Raj:	P – A – T – E – L .

2

Woman:	What's your address, Raj?
Raj:	It's 16 Market Road.
Woman:	16 Market Road ... OK.

3

Woman:	And what's your phone number?
Raj:	It's 960 8949.
Woman:	Great! Welcome to the club! Here's your card.
Raj:	Thanks!

2 **Complete the greetings with *morning*, *afternoon* or *evening*.**

1 Good ....!

2 Good ....!

3 Good ....!

3 (1/26) **Match the questions with the answers. Then listen and check.**

1 What's your name?
2 How do you spell that?
3 What's your address?
4 What's your phone number?

a It's 27 Baker Street.
b A – N – T – O – N – I – O.
c It's 371 8922.
d It's Antonio.

> **Your turn**
>
> **4** **Use the phrases in English today to write a dialogue. Act it out.**
>
> **Student A:** You are a new member of the sports club. Answer the questions.
> **Student B:** You are a sports coach. Greet the new member and ask for personal information.
>
> **A:** *Good afternoon. I'm here for the football club.*   **B:** *OK. What's your name?*

Writing: Complete a form

5 **Read the jumbled information about Batman and Iron Man. Complete the DVD club membership forms.**

1

DVD Club Membership
Name: *Bruce Wayne* ....
Address: ....
....
....
....
Phone: ....

1-800-IRONMAN

Stark Towers

Bat Phone

~~Bruce Wayne~~

Tony Stark

Gotham City

New York

Wayne Manor

2

DVD Club Membership
Name: ....
Address: ....
....
....
....
Phone: ....

> **Your turn**
>
> **6** **Make your own club membership form.**
>
> 1 Think of a club or invent one.
> 2 Design a membership form. Include:
>   • Name   • Address
>   • Age   • Phone number
> 3 Make copies. Ask and answer with your partner to complete the form.
> 4 Complete the form for you.

> Now turn to page 22 in the Activity Book.

MY FAVOURITE THINGS!

TOP THINGS FOR TODAY'S TEENAGERS

In the UK	In the USA
1 games console	1 games console
2 bike	2 skateboard
3 mobile phone	3 laptop
4 football shirt	4 baseball glove
5 pet (cat/dog/fish)	5 book

1

Hello! My name's Stuart and I'm from Cambridge in the UK. My favourite thing is my games console. My next favourite thing is my black and yellow football shirt. Cambridge United is my favourite team and yellow is my favourite colour!
Stuart, 10, Cambridge

2

Hi! I'm Britney and I'm from Santa Cruz in the USA. This is my favourite thing. It's a book. It's *War Horse* by Michael Morpurgo and it's great! My next favourite thing is my laptop. It's cool!
Britney, 10, Santa Cruz

3

Hi! I'm Suzanne and I'm from Glasgow in the UK. My favourite thing is my pet fish. His name's Nemo. He's white and orange. He's very funny. My next favourite thing is my bike. It's great.
Suzanne, 10, Glasgow

New words
baseball glove   cat   dog   fish
football shirt   games console
laptop   next   pet   team

Reading

1 **Listen and read.**

Comprehension

2 **Read the sentences and write the names.**

1 My favourite thing is a book. ....
2 My favourite thing is my fish. ....
3 My favourite thing is my games console.

....

3 **Read the text again and answer.**

1 What colour is the fish?
   He's white and orange.
2 What's black and yellow?
3 Where's Suzanne from?
4 Is Britney from the UK?
5 What's her next favourite thing?

Listening

4 **Listen to Lucy from Newcastle and tick (✓) the correct picture.**

1 Her pet is a:

 A ☐    B ☐

2 His name's:

 A ☐    B ☐

3 Her favourite thing is a:

 A ☐    B ☐

Speaking

5 **Ask your partner about his/her favourite thing or pet.**

A: *What's your favourite thing?*
B: *It's my bike.*
A: *What colour is it?*
B: *It's blue and white. What's your favourite thing?*
A: *It's my pet cat. His name's Tabby.*
B: *What colour is he?*
A: *He's grey and white.*

Project: My favourite things

6 **Find photos of your favourite thing or pet. Write about you and make a poster.**

Hi! My name's Carla and I'm from Milan in Italy. My favourite thing is my pet dog. Her name's Ellie. She's brown and white. My next favourite thing is my mobile phone. It's purple.

E Revision

1 **Look and write the possessions.**

1 *camera* ....
2 ....
3 ....
4 ....
5 ....
6 ....
7 ....
8 ....
9 ....
10 ....

Come on, kids! Let's tidy the garage.

2 **Look at the pictures and the word prompts. Ask and answer.**

1 **A:** *What colour is your jacket? Is it green?*
   B: *No, it isn't. It's brown.*

1 jacket / green

2 notebook / yellow

3 pencil case / blue

4 comic / orange

5 pen / black

6 eraser / pink

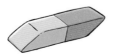

3 **Write the words under the correct bags.**

~~apple~~ ~~bike~~ dictionary eraser football
ice cream jacket notebook pen ruler
skateboard umbrella

a

an

bike ....
....
....
....
....
....
....
....

apple ....
....
....
....

4 **Cover Exercise 3. A: Say a word. B: Say *a* or *an*.**

A: *apple*
B: *an apple*

5 Game: A: Think of an object. B: Ask questions. Guess the object.

A: *I'm ready now!*
B: *Is it a pencil case?*
A: *No, it isn't.*
B: *Is it a bag?*
A: *Yes, it is.*
B: *Is it blue?*
A: *Yes, it is.*
B: *Is it my bag?*
A: *Yes!*

6 **1 29** Complete the dialogue with sentences a–f. Listen and check. Then act out the dialogue.

Man: Good afternoon! Are you here for the computer club?
Lily: ¹ *Yes, I am.*
Man: Great. What's your name?
Lily: ² ....
Man: How do you spell 'Lily'?
Lily: ³ ....
Man: What's your address, Lily?
Lily: ⁴ ....
Man: OK. And what's your phone number?
Lily: ⁵ ....
Man: Great! Welcome to the club! Here's your card.
Lily: ⁶ ....

a Thanks!
b It's 960 9894.
c It's Lily Baker.
d ~~Yes, I am.~~
e It's 14 Market Road.
f L – I – L – Y.

Rap: My things

7 **1 30** Listen and complete. Then listen and rap.

This is a ¹ *notebook* .
This is a book.
This is a ² ....
Look, look, look!
This is my ³ ....
It's really cool.
And this is a bag.
It's time for school!
This is a ⁴ ....
It's black and white.
This is a ⁵ ....
This is a ⁶ ....
This is the park for everyone.
Come on, come on! Let's have some fun!

Pronunciation: /b/

8 **1 31** Listen and repeat.
My **b**ag is **b**rown, my **b**ike is **b**lack,
My **b**ook is **b**lue – Hey, **b**ird! Come **b**ack!

My progress

9 Read and tick (✓).

I can:	
ask and answer about possessions. *What's this? It's a book.*	☐
talk about colours. *What colour is it? It's red.*	☐
ask and answer about everyday objects. *Is it a pen? No, it isn't, it's a pencil.*	☐
give personal information. *My address is 18 Market Road ...*	☐

> Turn to Unit 2 Check in the Activity Book on page 23.

GOAL!

Will Jones

Sasha Jones

Mr Jones

Wayne Beckman

Carlo Signori

Joe Redman

8 Good afternoon. What's your name?

My name's Will Jones.

9 My name's Carlo Signori. Your son's a very good goalkeeper. This is my phone number. Call me this evening, Mr Jones.

Brilliant!   You *are* great, Will! Well done!

New words

Bad luck.   Brilliant!   Call me.
cup final   goalkeeper   game   Goal!
Have fun!   son

Reading

1 (1/32) **Listen and read.**

Comprehension

2 **Answer *True* (✓) or *False* (✗).**

1 Wayne Beckman is great.   ✓
2 The London Schools' Cup Final is a big game.   ☐
3 Joe is from London United Football Club.   ☐
4 Carlo Signori is from London United.   ☐

3 **Match the people with the sentences.**

1 Bad luck.   `c`

2 Your son's a very good goalkeeper.   ☐

3 He's Wayne Beckman.   ☐

4 It's a big game but have fun!   ☐

5 Yes!!! It's a goal!   ☐

6 You're great too, Will.   ☐

a Carlo Signori	**d** Wayne
b Coach	**e** Sasha
c ~~Mr Jones~~	**f** Will

4 **Learn the story and act it out.**

3 Wild world

A Is he hungry?

Presentation

1 (33) **Listen and read.**

Keeper: Here are the penguins. This is Archie. He's an African penguin.

Robbie: Hello, Archie!

Lily: What's the matter with Archie? Is he cold?

Keeper: No, he isn't.

Lily: Is he hungry?

Keeper: Yes, he is. Here's his lunch. It's fish.

Lily: Look at Archie. He's happy now!

Robbie: Lucky Archie! *I'm* hungry now.

Lily: How about a fish, Robbie?

Robbie: Yuck! No thanks! *I'm* not a penguin!

2 (34) **Listen and repeat the dialogue.**

English today

• What's the matter (with Archie)?
• Look at (Archie).
• Lucky (Archie)!
• How about (a fish)?
• Yuck!

26

Vocabulary: Feelings

3 **Listen and repeat. Then match.**

| cold | happy | hot | hungry | ill |
| sad | thirsty | tired |

1 *hot*

1 Zack

2 Nicolas

3 Jenny

4 Mark

5 Simon

6 Kate

7 Mia

8 Kelly

4 **Look at pictures 1–7 in Exercise 3. Ask and answer.**

1 **A:** *What's the matter with Zack?*
B: *He's hot.*

5 **A: Choose a feeling from Exercise 3 and mime. B: Ask. A: Answer.**
B: *What's the matter?*
A: *I'm hungry.*

Grammar

Is he/she cold?
Yes, he/she **is**.
No, he/she **isn't**.

6 **Complete the dialogues. Ask and answer.**

1 **A:** Is he tired?
B: Yes, he *is* .

2 **A:** Is she hot?
B: No, she _____.

3 **A:** Is he happy?
B: _____.

4 **A:** _____ cold?
B: _____.

7 **Listen and match the people with the feelings.**

1	Raj	**a**	tired
2	Asha	**b**	happy
3	Alex	**c**	hot
4	Robbie	**d**	sad
5	Lily	**e**	cold

Speaking

8 **Look at Exercise 7. Ask and answer.**

1 **A:** *Is Raj sad?*
B: *No, he isn't. He's happy.*

1 sad **2** hot **3** ill **4** tired **5** happy

> Now turn to Unit 3A in the Activity Book. Start on page 24.

B Where are you from?

Lesson aim:
• ask and say where people are from

Presentation

1 **Listen and read.**

Lily:	That's a nice photo. Who are they?
Raj:	They're my grandparents.
Lily:	Are they from India?
Raj:	Yes, they are. They're from Mumbai.
Lily:	Really? Cool! And are you and Asha from India, too?
Raj:	No, we aren't. We're from the UK. Mum's from India but Dad's from London. Where are you from?
Lily:	Alex and I are from the UK, too.
Raj:	And Robbie?
Lily:	Robbie? Oh, he's from Mars!

2 **Listen and repeat the dialogue.**

Vocabulary: Countries

3 **Listen and repeat. Then find the countries.**

Argentina	Australia	India	Italy	Poland	Spain	the UK	the USA

1 *the USA*

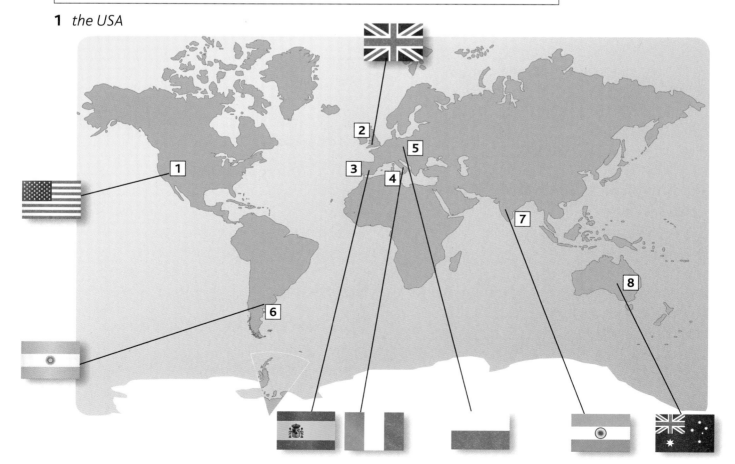

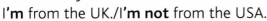

Grammar

Are you from India?
Yes, I **am**./No, **I'm** not.
Where **are** you from?
I**'m** from the UK./I**'m not** from the USA.

Grammar

We**'re** from Italy. They **aren't** from Poland.
Are you from India?
Yes, **we are**./No, **we aren't**.
Are they from the UK?
Yes, **they are**./No, **they aren't**.
Where **are you/they** from?

Speaking

4 Look at Exercise 3 again. A: Describe the national flag. B: Say the country.

A: *The flag is blue and white.*
B: *Is it Argentina?*
A: *Yes, it is.*

5 Imagine you are these people. Answer the questions. Then ask and answer with your partner.

Lionel Messi: Argentina

1 Are you from Poland?

No, I'm not. I'm from Argentina.

Prince William: the UK

2 Are you from the USA?

....

Penelope Cruz: Spain

3 Where are you from?

....

Katy Perry: the USA

4 Where are you from?

....

Listening

6 🔘 **1 40** Listen and choose where the people are from.

1 Robert is from *the USA / the UK*.
2 Marta is from *Poland / Italy*.
3 David and Carlos are from *Spain / Portugal*.

Speaking

7 Ask and answer about Tiki and Ronde Barber. Use the words in the box.

sisters/brothers   from the UK/from the USA
basketball players/football players

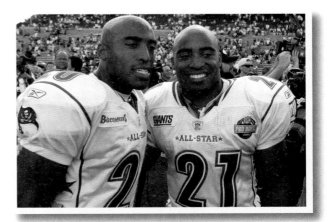

Ronde and Tiki Barber

A: *Are they sisters?*
B: *No, they aren't. They're brothers.*

Writing

8 Write about Tiki and Ronde Barber.

Tiki and Ronde Barber are ...

> Now turn to Unit 3B in the Activity Book. Start on page 28.

C The parrots are amazing!

Lesson aim:
• talk about wild animals

Presentation

1 🎧 1/41 **Listen and read.**

OUR TRIP TO THE ZOO!
by Robbie Baker

LOOK AT THE PHOTOS FROM OUR TRIP TO THE ZOO!

The ostriches are cute. Look at their faces!

The elephants are thirsty. They're very funny! Elephants are my favourite animals.

The parrots are red, blue, green and yellow. They're from Argentina. They're amazing!

And who are they? They aren't animals! That's my brother, Alex and my sister, Lily!

Vocabulary: Wild animals

2 🎧 1/42 **Listen and repeat. Ask and answer.**

crocodile   elephant   giraffe   lion   monkey   ostrich   parrot   polar bear   snake   zebra

A: *What animal is number one?*
B: *It's a parrot.*

Grammar

One	Two or more
one elephant	two elephant**s**
one giraffe	two giraffe**s**
one ostrich	two ostrich**es**

3 **1 43** **Listen and match.**

1 *B*

4 **Now write about their favourite animals.**

Robbie: His favourite animals are elephants.
Lily:
Alex:
Asha:

Grammar

Look at the photos from **our** trip.
Look at **their** faces.

5 **Complete the text. Write *our* or *their*.**

ANiMAL ADVENTURE!

by Barry and Sue the zookeepers

London Zoo is a very big zoo with lots of animals. Animal Adventure is ¹...*our*....... new children's zoo. Here are ²............... meerkats. They're ³............... favourite animals. ⁴............... fur is brown and ⁵............... faces are very cute. The meerkats are very happy in ⁶............... new home. Come and meet ⁷............... animals and have a wonderful time at Animal Adventure!

About you

6 **Now draw and write about your favourite animals.**

My name's Karen. My favourite animals are monkeys. They're funny and their faces are really cute!

monkey

> Now turn to Unit 3C in the Activity Book. Start on page 32.

D Revision

1 **Match the words with the people in the picture.**
Then point, ask and answer.

cold	hot	hungry	ill	sad	thirsty	tired

1 *hot*
A: *What's the matter with Miss Hooper?*
B: *She's hot.*

2 **Write the countries.**

1 the UK
2 ....
3 ....
4 ....
5 ....
6 ....
7 ....
8 ....

1 ~~het KU~~	5 eht AUS
2 suarAlati	6 tylaI
3 donlaP	7 enarAngit
4 naSip	8 ianId

3 **Complete the puzzle and find the mystery animal.**

4 Complete the sentences. Use the words in the box. Then ask and answer.

| am | 're | ~~Are~~ | aren't | are | Are | Are |

A: [1] _Are_ you from India?
B: Yes, I [2] ....

A: [3] .... you from Poland?
B: Yes, we [4] ....

A: [5] .... they from the UK?
B: No, they [6] ....
They [7] .... from the USA.

5 Play the game.

A: *Three snakes.*
B: *It's picture A!*

Song: We are at the zoo

6 🎵 1/44 Listen and complete. Then listen and sing.

It's a busy day today
We're keepers at the [1] _zoo_ .
Here's lunch for the polar bears
And for the kangaroo.
The [2] .... are amazing.
They're very scary, too.
Tigers, bears and [3] ....
It's great fun at the zoo.
All our favourite animals
Are right here at the zoo.
The elephants are [4] ....
And they're very thirsty, too.
Look at all the [5] .... here.
They're red and green and blue.
Zebras, snakes and tall [6] ....
It's great fun at the zoo!

Pronunciation: /s/

7 🎵 1/45 Listen and repeat.

Seven **s**illy monkeys
And **s**ix **s**ad **s**nake**s**.
Seven yummy i**c**e creams
And **s**ix **s**mall cake**s**.

My progress

8 Read and tick (✓).

I can:	
ask and talk about feelings. *What's the matter?* *I'm hungry.* *What's the matter with Alex?* *He's hungry.*	☐
ask and say where people are from. *Where are you from?* *I'm from the UK.*	☐
talk about wild animals. *My favourite animals are monkeys.*	☐

> Turn to Unit 3 Check in the Activity Book on page 36.

pick and mix

Fun Time!

What animal is it? Look and write.

crocodile   elephant   giraffe   lion
~~parrot~~   snake

1 *parrot*

2 _____

3 _____

4 _____

5 _____

6 _____

Guess what?

Read the facts. Match the animals with their tracks.

AMAZING ANIMALS!

1 Is a zebra black with white stripes, or white with black stripes? The answer is, it's white with black stripes.

2 This is a polar bear. Its fur isn't white. It's clear, like glass.

3 Adult giraffes are about six metres tall. Baby giraffes are about two metres tall.

A

B

C

STAR SPOT

Kristen Stewart

Favourite bands: Green Day and The Beatles
Favourite sport: surfing

This is Kristen Stewart. She's from California in the USA. Her dad is from the USA but her mum is from Australia.

Kristen is a famous actress. She's famous for her *Twilight* films. Kristen's favourite things are books and films. Her favourite colours are red and blue. Kristen is an animal lover, too. Her three dogs, Oz, Jack and Lily, and her cat, Jella, are very happy about that!

Read and match.

1 Kristen is
2 Her mum is from
3 Green Day is
4 *Twilight* is
5 Oz is
6 Her favourite colours are

a a dog.
b a film.
c red and blue.
d a band.
e an actress.
f Australia.

JUST **JOKING!**

What's big and grey, with four wheels?

An elephant on a skateboard!

How to ... draw a lion!

Step 1: Draw three ovals and four circles.

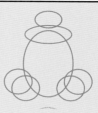

Step 2: Draw six lines.

Step 3: Draw the head parts.

Step 4: Draw the face. Erase the pencil lines.

Step 5: Colour your lion.

4 In my room

A It's Lily's T-shirt.

Lesson aim:
- identify people's clothes

1

3

2

4

5

Presentation

1 🔊 1/46 **Listen and read.**

Robbie: Where are my jeans?

Lily: I don't know.

Mum: They're here. What's this? Is it your T-shirt, Robbie?

Robbie: No way! It's pink. It's Lily's T-shirt.

Mum: Sorry! And this is your dress, Lily. But where are your white jeans?

Lily: They're here. Wow! Your shoes are huge, Robbie!

Robbie: These aren't *my* shoes. These are *Dad's* shoes! They're size 44!

2 🔊 1/47 **Listen and repeat the dialogue.**

> **English today!**
>
> - I don't know.
> - No way!

Vocabulary: Clothes

3 **1 48** **Listen and repeat. Then match.**

| dress hat jacket jeans jumper
shoe(s) skirt trainer(s) trousers
T-shirt |

1 *hat*

4 **Look at the clothes in Exercise 3.
Ask and answer.**

A: *What's number one?*
B: *It's a hat. What's number eight?*
A: *They're jeans.*

Grammar
It's Lily**'s** T-shirt.
They're Dad**'s** shoes.

Speaking

5 **Look at the photo on page 36.
Ask and answer.**

A: *What's number one?*
B: *It's Mrs Baker's jumper.*
A: *What colour is it?*
B: *It's blue.*

Grammar
What's **this**?

This is your dress.

These are Dad's shoes.

6 **Talk about your clothes and your
partner's clothes.**

This is my T-shirt and these are my jeans.
This is Jarek's jacket and these are his trainers.

Speaking

7 **Look at the people in Exercise 3 and ask
and answer about their clothes.**

1 A: *What's this?*
B: *It's Jack's hat. It's purple.*

About you

8 **Draw you and a friend. Write about
your clothes.**

*This is me in my favourite clothes.
This is my favourite T-shirt. It's green.
And these are my jeans. They're blue.*

*This is my friend, Roberto. Roberto's
jacket is red and his jeans are black.
They're his favourite clothes.*

> Now turn to Unit 4A in the Activity Book. Start on page 37.

B Is he under the bed?

Presentation

1 **Listen and read.**

At Grandad's house. The children are playing 'Hide and seek'.

Lily: ...18 ... 19 ... 20! Here I come! Robbie! You're in the cupboard.

Robbie: No, I'm not.

Lily: Yes, you are. Don't be silly!

Robbie: Oh, OK. Now, where's Alex?

Later ...

Robbie: He isn't in the living room and he isn't in the bathroom.

Lily: He's here! He's in the bedroom.

Robbie: Where is he? Is he under the bed?

Lily: No, he's in the bed, under the duvet.

Robbie: Alex! What's the matter? Are you tired?

2 **Listen and repeat the dialogue.**

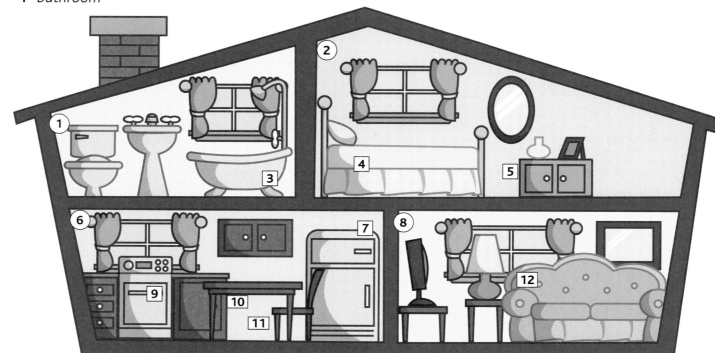

English today
- Here I come!
- Don't be silly!

Vocabulary: Rooms and furniture

3 **Listen and repeat. Then match.**

Rooms:	bathroom bedroom kitchen living room
Furniture:	bath bed chair cooker cupboard fridge sofa table

1 *bathroom*

Grammar

Where's the cat?

It's **in** the box.   It's **on** the box.

It's **under** the box.

Listening

4 (1/52) **Listen and tick (✓) the correct pictures. Then say where the people are.**

1 Where's Robbie?
He's in the bathroom.

2 Where's Asha?

3 Where's Raj?

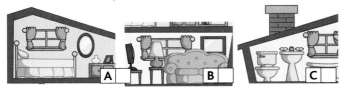

4 Where's Lily?

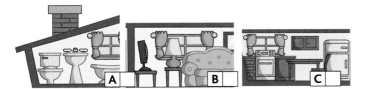

5 **Look at Exercise 4 again. Ask and answer.**

1 A: *Is Robbie in the bedroom?*
   B: *No, he isn't. He's in the bathroom.*

1 Robbie / bedroom
2 Asha / kitchen
3 Raj / bedroom
4 Lily / kitchen

6 **Look at the picture. Ask and answer.**

1 A: *Where's the cake?*
   B: *It's on the table.*

1 cake
2 apple
3 hat
4 book
5 umbrella

Game

7 **B: Look at the picture in Exercise 6. Choose an object. A: Ask and answer. Guess the object.**

A: *Is it on the chair?*
B: *No, it isn't.*
A: *Is it under the table?*
B: *Yes, it is.*
A: *It's the umbrella!*
B: *That's right!*

> Now turn to Unit 4B in the Activity Book. Start on page 41.

Communication

Speaking: Look for things

1 DVD 1/53 **Listen and read.**

Asha and Lily are at the swimming pool.

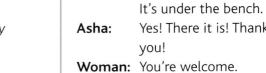

1

Asha: Oh no! Where's my jacket?
Lily: What's it like?
Asha: It's blue.
Lily: Hmm ... It isn't on the bench ...
Asha: Oh no! It's lost!

2

Lily: Look, Asha! Is this your jacket?
Woman: No, it isn't! It's *my* jacket!
Lily: Oh! Sorry!
Woman: That's OK.

3

Woman: Is your jacket blue? It's under the bench.
Asha: Yes! There it is! Thank you!
Woman: You're welcome.

2 1/54 **Complete the dialogue. Listen and check.**

| lost | ~~Where~~ | Thank | Sorry | welcome | What's |

Oh no! Where's my jumper?

Robbie: Oh no! ¹ *Where* 's my jumper?
Raj: ² .... it like?
Robbie: It's red.
Raj: OK. Hmm ... It isn't on the sofa ...
Robbie: Oh no! It's ³ ....!
Raj: Look, Robbie! Is this your jumper?
Lily: No, it isn't. It's *my* jumper.
Raj: Oh! ⁴ ....!
Lily: That's OK.
Mum: Is your jumper red? It's in your bedroom.
Robbie: Yes! There it is! ⁵ .... you!
Mum: You're ⁶ ....

English today

Look for things

- Where's my ... ?
- What's it like?
- It's lost!
- There it is!
- Thank you!
- You're welcome.

3 **1 55** **Listen and choose the correct places. Then ask and answer.**

1 A: *Where's my mobile phone?*
   B: *It's on the sofa.*

1 on the sofa / under the chair

2 in the cupboard / on the table

3 under the bed / under the desk

Your turn

4 **Use the phrases in English today to write a dialogue. Act it out.**

Student A: Your favourite T-shirt is lost.
Student B: Ask your friend questions to find it.
Student C: You find the T-shirt. Say where it is.

A: *Oh no! Where's my ... ?*
B: *What's ... ?*

Writing: Find a lost pet

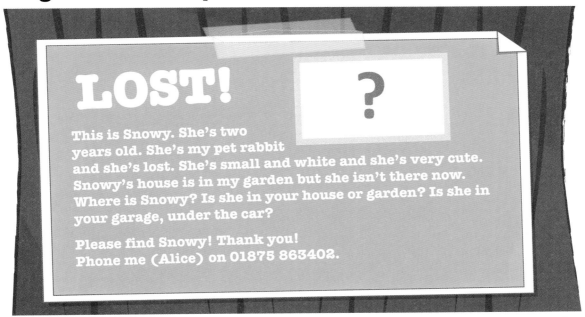

LOST!

?

This is Snowy. She's two years old. She's my pet rabbit and she's lost. She's small and white and she's very cute. Snowy's house is in my garden but she isn't there now. Where is Snowy? Is she in your house or garden? Is she in your garage, under the car?

Please find Snowy! Thank you!
Phone me (Alice) on 01875 863402.

5 **Read the poster. Which rabbit is Snowy?**

1

2

3

6 **Read the poster and answer the questions.**

1 What type of animal is the pet? *It's a rabbit.*
2 What's the problem?
3 How old is Snowy?
4 What colour is Snowy?
5 Where's Snowy's house?

Your turn

7 **Imagine that your pet is lost. Make a poster to find your pet.**

1 Find or draw a picture of your pet.
2 Make your poster. Draw or stick a picture of your pet on the poster.
3 Write about your pet. Include a phone number.

> Now turn to page 45 in the Activity Book.

BEDROOMS IN THE UK

These are typical homes in the UK. In a typical home, there are two or three bedrooms. A lot of bedrooms are for two children. Their beds are often bunk beds — one bed under the other. They're really fun!

flats

terraced houses

1

My name's Kavya. My parents are from India but my home is in Bristol in the UK. This is my room. Well, it's Nadia's room, too — she's my sister. Our room is small but it's cosy. My computer is on the desk. The bunk beds are really cool! My bedroom is my favourite room in the house.
Kavya, 11, Bristol

2

I'm George and I'm from Newcastle. This isn't my bedroom. It's my brother's room. His name's Toby. His clothes aren't in the wardrobe. They're on the bed and on a chair. His posters are on the floor. My brother's bedroom is a mess! The clothes in my room are in the wardrobe. My room is tidy!
George, 10, Newcastle

New words

bunk beds   cosy   desk   floor
mess   poster   small   tidy
wardrobe

Reading

1 (1/56) **Listen and read.**

Comprehension

2 **Read the texts again. Match the objects with the rooms.**

1 a wardrobe ....*b*....
2 posters ....
3 a computer ....
4 bunk beds ....

a Kavya's bedroom
b George's brother's bedroom

3 **Read and answer *True (✓)* or *False (x)*.**

Kavya

1 My room isn't small. ☒
2 My computer is on the desk. ☐

George

3 My bedroom is tidy. ☐
4 My brother's clothes are in his wardrobe. ☐

Listening

4 (1/57) **Listen to Alice and choose the correct answers.**

1 She's from (Cardiff)/ Bristol.
2 It's *Alice's / Alice and Jane's* bedroom.
3 Jane's bed is *blue / yellow*.
4 A *TV / computer* is in their bedroom.

Speaking

5 **Ask and answer about your bedroom.**

A: *What's your bedroom like?*
B: *It's small but it's cosy.*
A: *What's in your room?*
B: *A desk, a computer ...*

Project: My room

6 **Write about your room and make a poster.**

Hi! My name's Bartek and I'm from Poznan in Poland. My room is great. It's my brother's room, too.
My brother's computer is on the desk. My clothes are on the floor but my brother's clothes are in the wardrobe. He's very tidy but I'm not!

E Revision

1 **Label the clothes. Then point and say.**

1 *It's a dress.*   **2** *They're trousers.*

3 _____

5 _____

8 _____

1 *dress* _____

2 *trousers* _____

4 _____

6 _____

7 _____

2 **Look at the picture. Choose the correct words. Then ask and answer.**

1 The sofa is in the *living room / (kitchen.)*
A: *Where's the sofa?*
B: *It's in the kitchen.*
2 The *bath / bed* is in the living room.
3 The *cupboard / cooker* is in the bedroom.
4 The fridge is in the *kitchen / bathroom*.
5 The *cooker / bed* is in the bathroom.
6 The *cooker / cupboard* is in the living room.

3 **Draw your house and talk about it.**

The sofa is in the living room …

4 **Find and write.**

1 ___*It's Lisa's*___ jumper.
2 _____ trainers.
3 _____ jeans.
4 _____ hat.

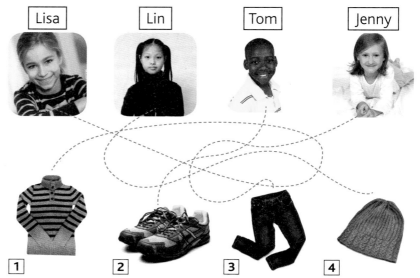

5 Write *in*, *on* or *under*. Then ask your partner to close his or her book and play a guessing game.

1 The books are ___in___ the cupboard.
A: *They're in the cupboard.*
B: *The books!*

2 The bags are _____ the table.
3 The mobile phone is _____ the chair.
4 The photos are _____ the cupboard.
5 The camera is _____ the table.
6 The ruler is _____ the bag.

6 🔊 1/58 Complete the dialogue. Listen and check. Then act out the dialogue.

Asha: Oh no! [1] __Where's__ my hat?
Lily: What's it like?
Asha: It's [2] _____.
Lily: OK. Hmm ... It isn't under the bed ...
Asha: Oh no! It's [3] _____.
Lily: Look, Asha! Is this your hat?
Raj: No, it [4] _____. It's *my* hat.
Lily: Oh! [5] _____!
Raj: That's OK.
Robbie: Is your hat black? It's in the living room.
Asha: Yes! There it is! Thank you!
Robbie: You're [6] _____.

1	**A** What's	**B** ~~Where's~~	**C** Who's
2	**A** black	**B** sad	**C** tired
3	**A** orange	**B** happy	**C** lost
4	**A** isn't	**B** is	**C** aren't
5	**A** Hello	**B** Sorry	**C** Cool
6	**A** lost	**B** nice	**C** welcome

Rap: Where's my blue hat?

7 🔊 1/59 Listen and complete. Then listen and rap.

Where's my blue [1] __hat__?
Where, oh where?
It isn't on the [2] _____.
It isn't on the chair.
It isn't on the table.
Or [3] _____ my bed.
Oh, silly me!
It's on my head!
Where's my [4] _____?
Where, oh where?
It isn't in my [5] _____.
It isn't here or there.
It isn't in the [6] _____.
It's lost — oh dear!
Oh, silly me!
My jumper's here!

Pronunciation: /ð/

8 🔊 1/60 Listen and repeat.

Who are **th**ey? Who's **th**is? Who's **th**at?
They're my bro**th**ers, Dan and Matt
And **th**at's my mo**th**er wi**th th**e cat!

My progress

9 Read and tick (✓).

I can:	
identify people's clothes. *It's Lily's T-shirt.*	☐
ask and say where people and things are. A: *Is Robbie in the bathroom?* B: *No, he isn't. He's in the bedroom.* A: *Is it on the chair?* B: *No, it isn't.*	☐
look for things. *Oh no! Where's my jacket? It's lost!*	☐

> Turn to Unit 4 Check in the Activity Book on page 46.

Where's Sparky?

Amy

Mrs Morris

Mum   Dad   Sparky

6 I'm sorry, Mrs Morris. Sparky isn't in our garden.

Poor Sparky! He's lost.

7 Later ...

Oh look! It's Mrs Morris's cat! Sparky!

Dad! Sparky's here! He's in my room!

8 It's OK, Mrs Morris. Here's Sparky!

Oh thank you, Amy.

You're welcome!

THE END

New words

car   doorbell   storm   tree

Reading

1 🔊 1 61 **Listen and read.**

Comprehension

2 **Match the sentences with the people.**

1 I'm sorry, Mrs Morris.   **a** Amy
2 Look at the storm!   **b** Mrs Morris
3 Sparky's my friend.   **c** Dad
4 Poor Sparky!   **d** Mum

3 **Learn the story and act it out.**

5 People and pets

A Have you got a torch?

Presentation

1 **Listen and read.**

The Baker family are on a camping holiday.

Diane: Hi, I'm Diane. I'm in the next tent.

Lily: Cool. I'm Lily.

Diane: We've got a problem with our tent. Have you got a torch?

Lily: Yes, I have. Here you are.

Diane: Great, thanks!

Robbie: Oh no!

Lily: That's my brother, Robbie. What's the matter, Robbie?

Robbie: My CD player's broken.

Diane: Let me look. It isn't broken. You haven't got a CD in it!

Lily: Typical!

2 **Listen and repeat the dialogue.**

English today

· Here you are.
· Let me look.
· Typical!

Vocabulary: Possessions (2)

3 (1/64) **Listen and repeat. Then point, ask and answer.**

> a CD player   an MP3 player
> a pair of sunglasses   a sleeping bag
> a tent   a torch   a watch

A: *What's number one?*
B: *It's a pair of sunglasses.*

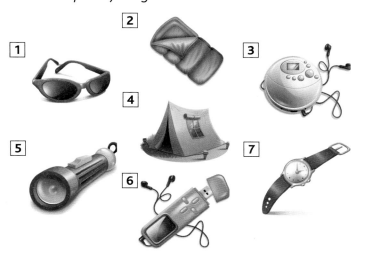

Grammar

I**'ve got** a torch.
I **haven't got** a torch.
You**'ve got** sunglasses.
You **haven't got** a CD.
Have you **got** a torch?
Yes, I **have.**/No, I **haven't.**

I've got = I have got
I haven't got = I have not got

4 **You are DJ Danny. Say what you have/haven't got. Use prompts 1–6.**

1 *I've got an MP3 player.*

1 an MP3 player
2 a sleeping bag
3 a watch
4 a tent
5 a torch
6 a pair of sunglasses

Speaking

5 **A: Ask DJ Danny questions. B: You are DJ Danny. Answer the questions.**

A: *Have you got an MP3 player?*
B: *Yes, I have.*

Listening

6 (1/65) **Listen to the people. Tick (✓) what they've got.**

Name	Possessions
Sunita	1 ✓ 2 3
Simon	4 5 6
Nikki	7 8 9

7 **You are Sunita, Simon or Nikki. Say what you've got.**

I'm Sunita. I've got a torch and a ...

Writing

8 **Look at the things in Exercise 3. Write what you have/haven't got at home.**

1 *I've got a pair of sunglasses.*
2 *I haven't got a sleeping bag.*

> Now turn to Unit 5A in the Activity Book. Start on page 47.

B He's got short blonde hair.

Lesson aim:
• describe people

Presentation

1 **Listen and read.**

Lily:	Excuse me.
Man:	Hello. What's the matter?
Lily:	My little brother is lost. His name's Alex.
Man:	OK. What kind of hair has he got?
Lily:	He's got short blonde hair and he's got blue eyes.
Man:	Has he got glasses?
Lily:	No, he hasn't.
Woman:	Excuse me. Have you got a brother called Alex?
Lily:	Yes, I have.
Woman:	He's in our tent with my little boy.
Lily:	Phew! Thank you!

2  **Listen and repeat the dialogue.**

English today

• Excuse me.
• ... (a brother) called (Alex).
• Phew!

Vocabulary: Appearance

3 **Listen and repeat.**

Hair colour:	black blonde brown red
Hair length:	long medium-length short
Eye colour:	blue brown green grey

4 **Now complete the table.**

	Sandeep	Will	Sarah
Hair colour	1 _black_	5 _____	9 _____
Hair length	2 _____	6 _____	10 _____
Eye colour	3 _____	7 _____	11 _____
Glasses (yes/no)	4 _____	8 _____	12 _____

Grammar

What kind of hair **has** he/she **got**?

He**'s got** short blonde hair.

She **hasn't got** long blonde hair.

Has he/she **got** glasses?

Yes, he/she **has**.

No, he/she **hasn't**.

He/She's got = He/She has got

He/She hasn't got = He/She has not got

Speaking

5 **Describe the people in Exercise 4.**

Sandeep has got medium-length black hair and brown eyes. He hasn't got glasses.

6 **Look at the photos and ask and answer.**

Mr Baker   Mrs Baker

Lily   Robbie   Alex

1 A: *Has Mr Baker got blonde hair?*
   B: *No, he hasn't.*
   A: *What kind of hair has he got?*
   B: *He's got short brown hair.*

1 Mr Baker / blonde hair?
2 Lily / short hair?
3 Robbie / red hair?
4 Alex / brown hair?
5 Mrs Baker / short hair?

7 **Complete the sentences about the Baker family.**

1 Mr Baker *hasn't got* black hair.
2 Lily .... short hair.
3 Mrs Baker .... long hair.
4 Robbie .... blonde hair.
5 Alex .... curly hair.

8 **Ask and answer about a brother, sister or cousin.**

A: *Have you got a brother or sister?*

B: *Yes, I have. I've got a brother. His name's Diego.*

A: *What kind of hair has he got?*

B: *He's got short brown hair.*

9 **Describe someone in your class. Your classmates guess who it is.**

A: *This person has got short black hair and grey eyes.*

B: *Is it Luca?*

A: *Yes! That's right!*

About you

10 **Find a photo of a friend or someone in your family. Write about him or her.**

This is my cousin, Hakan. He's from Istanbul. He's fifteen years old. He's got short black hair and blue eyes.

> Now turn to Unit 5B in the Activity Book. Start on page 51.

C They've got lots of dogs!

Lesson aim:
• describe pets

Presentation

1 (2/01) **Listen and read.**

The Patels are at a dogs' home in London.

Asha: Wow! They've got lots of dogs here.
Raj: Have they got cats here, too?
Asha: No, they haven't Raj. This is a home for *dogs*!
Raj: This dog's very friendly, Dad.
Dad: Yes, but it's big. Look at its paws!
Raj: Please, Dad. We haven't got a pet.
Dad: Hmm, I'm not sure.
Asha: Robbie and Lily have got a dog.
Raj: And we've got a big garden ...
Dad: Maybe next year ...

2 (2/02) **Listen and repeat the dialogue.**

Vocabulary: Pets

3 (2/03) **Listen and repeat. Then label the picture below.**

| bird | cat | dog | fish | hamster | lizard | rabbit | tortoise |

English today

• ... lots of ...
• I'm not sure.
• Maybe.

Waiting room

A

4 ....

B

C

D

H

E

F

1 *dog* ....

G

3 ....

I

6 ....

J

8 ....

2 ....

5 ....

7 ....

Vocabulary: Parts of animals

4 (2 04) **Listen and repeat. Then match with A–J in Exercise 3.**

| body | ear | feet | foot | head | leg |
| nose | paw | tail | wing | | |

A *nose*

Grammar

They**'ve got** lots of dogs here.
The dogs **have got** big paws.
We **haven't got** a pet.
Have they **got** cats?
Yes, they **have**./No, they **haven't**.

We/They've got = We/They have got
We/They haven't got = We/They have not got

5 **Look at the pictures. Choose the correct words.**

1 *They've got / They haven't got* long ears.

2 *We've got / We haven't got* a cat.

3 *They've got / They haven't got* wings.

6 Write *have got, 've got* or *haven't got.*

I'm Ben and this is my sister, Katie. Our parents have got a farm. We ¹ *'ve got* lots of pets. We ² _____ three dogs. They ³ _____ long ears but they ⁴ _____ long tails. We ⁵ _____ two cats and two rabbits, too. The cats ⁶ _____ black tails and white paws. The rabbits ⁷ _____ black tails. Their tails are white. They ⁸ _____ long ears, too. Our pets are very friendly!

7 **Look at the picture in Exercise 6. Ask and answer.**

1 **A:** *Have Ben and Katie got two dogs?*
B: *No, they haven't. They've got three dogs.*

1 Ben and Katie / two dogs?
2 the dogs / short ears?
3 the cats / white tails?
4 the rabbits / long ears?

About you

8 Write about your favourite type of pet.

I love lizards!
Lizards are my favourite type of pet. Lizards are green or brown.
They're small and they've got long bodies. They've got long tails and they've got four short legs.

> Now turn to Unit 5C in the Activity Book. Start on page 55.

D Revision

1 Complete the possessions.

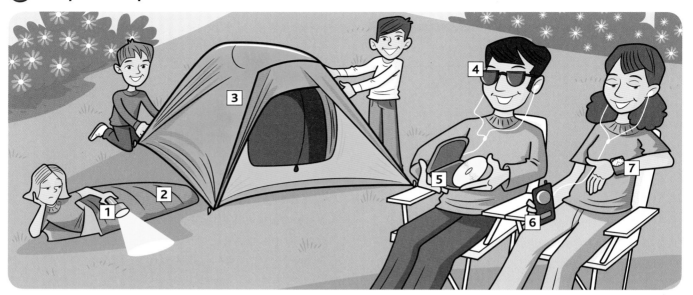

1 t o r c h
2 s _ ee _ n _ b _
3 _ en _
4 _ un _ as _ e _

5 _ D _ ay _ r
6 M _ pl _ y _
7 w _ t _ h

2 Write sentences. Then match.

A

B

C

1 brown / got / hair. / He's / short
   He's got short brown hair.   C

2 glasses. / brown / got / She's / and / eyes
   .... ☐

3 blue / She's / eyes. / got
   .... ☐

4 medium-length / hair. /got / grey / She's
   .... ☐

5 got / hair. / long / She's / blonde
   .... ☐

6 and / He's / glasses. / green eyes / got
   .... ☐

3 Unscramble the animal body parts.

1 wap *paw*   2 ngiw ....

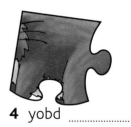

3 ital ....   4 yobd ....

5 sare ....   6 efte ....

7 ahde ....   8 soen ....

4 Look at the table and write sentences.

	Lucy	Fred	Mike and Sue
🐕	✗	✗	✓
🐈	✓	✓	✗
🐢	✗	✓	✓
🐹	✓	✗	✗

1 Lucy / hamster / tortoise
Lucy has got a hamster but she hasn't got a tortoise.

2 Fred / cat / tortoise

....

3 Mike and Sue / dog

....

4 Fred / tortoise / dog

....

5 Mike and Sue / hamster

....

6 Lucy / dog / cat

....

5 Look at Exercise 4. Ask and answer the questions with your partner.

1 Has Lucy got a tortoise?
No, she hasn't.
2 Have Mike and Sue got a hamster?
3 Have Mike and Sue got a dog?
4 Has Fred got a dog?
5 Has Lucy got a hamster?
6 Has Fred got a tortoise?

Song: We've got a funny pet

6 🎵 2 05 Listen and complete. Then listen and sing.

We've got a funny [1] ..*pet*........... .
It's from outer space.
It's got a purple body
And a big green [2] ....
It's got long ears
And a long tail, too.
It's got orange [3] ....
And its eyes are blue.
We've got a funny pet
And it's very sweet.
Its [4] .... is orange
And it's got big [5] ....
It hasn't got paws
And it hasn't got [6] ....
But it's cute and friendly,
Like a teddy bear!

Pronunciation: /ɒ/

7 🎵 2 06 Listen and repeat.

Tom's got a dog.
Her name is Dot.
Her body is long,
But her tail is not.

My progress

8 Read and tick (✓).

I can:	
ask and answer about possessions. A: *Have you got a torch?* B: *Yes, I have.*	☐
describe people. *She's got long blonde hair and blue eyes.*	☐
describe pets. *They've got black tails and white paws.*	☐

> Turn to Unit 5 Check in the Activity Book on page 59.

pick and mix

Guess what?

Read the facts and choose.

The glass lizard ¹*has / hasn't* got legs but it's a lizard, not a snake!

Dogs have got 42 teeth. Cats have got ²*30 / 50* teeth. You've got 32 teeth!

In the USA, white cats are ³*good / bad* luck and black cats are bad luck.

Dalmatians are a kind of dog. They're white with ⁴*red / black* spots. But Dalmatian puppies haven't got spots. They're just white.

JUST JOKING!

What kind of dog hasn't got a tail?

A hot dog!

What's got four eyes and eight legs?

Two giraffes!

Fun Time!

Look at the pictures. Find twelve differences.

In Picture A, the boys have got white T-shirts. In Picture B ... In Picture A, a cat is under the tree. In Picture B ...

A

B

STAR SPOT

Hania and her puppies

Read and answer *True* (✓) or *False* (✗).

This is Hania. She's six years old and she's from Warsaw, in Poland. She's a big black dog. She's got long ears, a long tail and very big paws. Hania is a star. She's mother to seventeen puppies! Hania has got eight male puppies and nine female puppies. They're all very cute!

1	Hania is five years old.	✗
2	Hania is from Poland.	
3	Hania has got small paws.	
4	Hania has got seventeen puppies.	
5	Hania has got nine male puppies.	
6	The puppies are very cute.	

6 Action!

A Don't laugh!

Presentation

① 🔊 2/07 **Listen and read.**

Lily: We're ready, Miss Carr.

Miss Carr: Good. Lily, sit down. Don't smile. You're sad in this play.

Lily: Sorry.

Miss Carr: Now Robbie, ring the doorbell. Raj, stand up and walk to the door but don't run. Excellent! Now, open the door.

Raj: Ha ha!

Miss Carr: Stop! Don't laugh, Raj!

Raj: But look at Robbie's helmet. It's really big!

Miss Carr: Don't be silly! Let's start again, everyone!

② 🔊 2/08 **Listen and repeat the dialogue.**

English today

• We're ready.
• Excellent!
• Let's start again, everyone!

Grammar

Stand up!
Stop!
Don't laugh!

Vocabulary: Action verbs

3 2 09 **Listen and repeat. Then match.**

Close the door!   Don't eat here!
Don't laugh!   Don't run!   Don't talk!
Listen to me!   Open the window!
Sit down!   Stand up!   Stop!

1 *Stand up!*

Listening

4 2 10 **Listen and follow the instructions.**

Stand up!

Speaking

5 A: **Give your partner instructions.**
B: **Follow the instructions.**

A: *Sit down!*

6 A: **Make a sentence with a word from column A. B: Choose a phrase from column B.**

A: *I'm tired.*
B: *Sit down!*

A	B
tired	Don't open the window!
sad	Sit down!
cold	Eat this apple!
hungry	Run!
late	Don't cry!

7 **Complete the school rules. Use the words in the box.**

Do   ~~Don't talk~~   Don't do   Listen   Talk

¹ *Don't talk* to your friends in your language! ² _____ to your friends in English! ³ _____ your homework in the evening. People are tired in the evening. ⁴ _____ your homework in the afternoon. ⁵ _____ to your teacher!

> Now turn to Unit 6A in the Activity Book. Start on page 60.

B Can you draw?

Lesson aim:
• talk about ability

Presentation

 1 Listen and read.

Lily:	It's Miss Carr's birthday on Sunday.
Asha:	Oh, OK. We can make a card for her. Can you draw?
Lily:	No. I can't draw but I can make a birthday card on my laptop. And I can make a cake.
Asha:	Wow! Can you cook?
Lily:	Yes, I can.
Robbie:	No, she can't!
Lily:	Robbie! What can *you* do?
Robbie:	I can sing. Listen!
Lily:	Stop, Robbie! You can't sing!

 2 Listen and repeat the dialogue.

Vocabulary: Activity verbs

 3 Listen and repeat. Then point to an activity. Ask and answer.

act	cook	dance	draw	make a cake	play football
play the guitar	ride a bike	sing	speak Spanish	swim	

A: *What's number one?*
B: *Sing*

4 A: Mime an activity. B: Guess what it is.

B: *Sing?*

A: *No! It's act.*

Grammar

I **can** make a cake.

I **can't** draw.

Can you cook?

Yes, I **can**.

No, I **can't**.

I can't = I cannot

Speaking

5 Look at the activity verbs in Exercise 3.
Ask and answer with your partner.

A: *Can you act?*

B: *Yes, I can.*

A: *Can you cook?*

B: *No, I can't.*

Writing

6 Write about Robbie, Lily, Raj and Asha.

Robbie can swim and play football but he can't dance or speak Spanish.

	Swim	Dance	Speak Spanish	Play football
	✓	✗	✗	✓
	✓	✓	✓	✗
	✓	✓	✗	✓
	✓	✓	✗	✗

Game

7 Look at the table in Exercise 6.
A: Choose a character. B: Guess who your partner is.

A: *I can play football, I can swim and I can dance but I can't speak Spanish.*

B: *You're Raj!*

A: *That's right! Now it's your turn!*

Listening

8 🔊 **2 14** Listen and tick (✓) what the people can do and cross (✗) what they can't do.

1 Marcus

A cook [✗]   B draw [ ]   C ride a bike [ ]

2 Julie

A act [ ]   B swim [ ]   C play football [ ]

3 Oliver

A sing [ ]   B play the guitar [ ]   C dance [ ]

About you

9 Write an email to Robbie, Lily, Raj or Asha about things you can do.

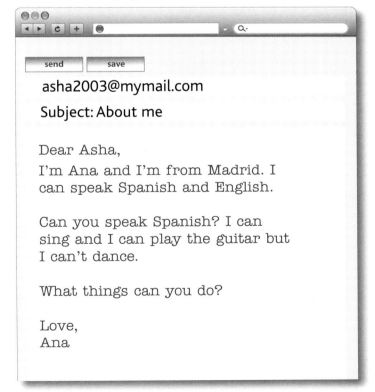

send   save

asha2003@mymail.com

Subject: About me

Dear Asha,
I'm Ana and I'm from Madrid. I can speak Spanish and English.

Can you speak Spanish? I can sing and I can play the guitar but I can't dance.

What things can you do?

Love,
Ana

> Now turn to Unit 6B in the Activity Book. Start on page 64.

Speaking: Make suggestions

1   **Listen and read.**

Robbie and Raj see a poster for the school talent competition.

1

Raj:	Hey, Robbie! Look at this!
Robbie:	A talent competition! Cool!
Raj:	Let's enter!
Robbie:	What can you do?

2

Raj:	I can play the guitar.
Robbie:	And I can sing!
Raj:	Let's start a band!
Robbie:	Good idea!

3

Robbie:	We can practise now!
Raj:	I can't. I'm busy.
Robbie:	Can you practise tomorrow?
Raj:	Yes, I can. Great!

English today

Make suggestions
- Let's (enter).
- We can (practise now).

Respond to suggestions
- Good idea!
- I can't. I'm busy.

2 **Complete the sentences.**

1 There's a _talent_ competition at school.
2 Raj can play the _____.
3 Robbie can _____.
4 Raj _____ practise now.
5 Robbie and Raj can _____ tomorrow.

3 2/16 **Choose the correct words. Then listen and check.**

Lily:	Hey, Asha! [1] (*Look*)/ *Listen* at this!
Asha:	A talent competition! Wow!
Lily:	[2] *We / Let's* enter!
Asha:	What [3] *are / can* you do?
Lily:	[4] *I / she* can dance.
Asha:	I can dance, too!
Lily:	Let's [5] *start / open* a dance group!
Asha:	Yes! [6] *Good / Bad* idea!
Lily:	Let's practise now!
Asha:	OK. We can practise in my garden.
Lily:	Great!

Your turn

4 **Use the phrases in** English today **to write a dialogue. Act it out.**

Student A: You want to enter the talent competition. Ask what your friend can do.
Student B: Answer your friend's questions and ask what he/she can do.

A: *Hey, ...! Look at this!*
B: *A talent competition! Cool!*

Writing: Start a club

5 **Read and complete the poster.**

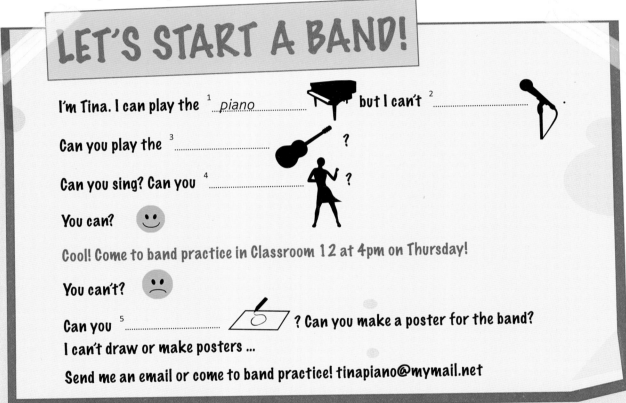

LET'S START A BAND!

I'm Tina. I can play the ¹ _piano_ but I can't ² ....

Can you play the ³ .... ?

Can you sing? Can you ⁴ .... ?

You can? 😊

Cool! Come to band practice in Classroom 12 at 4pm on Thursday!

You can't? 😞

Can you ⁵ .... ? Can you make a poster for the band?
I can't draw or make posters ...

Send me an email or come to band practice! tinapiano@mymail.net

6 **Read the poster and answer the questions.**

1 Can Tina sing?
   No, she can't.
2 Can Tina play the piano?
   ....
3 Where is band practice?
   ....
4 Can Tina draw?
   ....

Your turn

7 **Make a poster to start a sports club or a drama club.**

1 Choose a club. Use these questions to help you.
   • What kind of club is it?
   • Where is the club?
   • When is the club?
2 Think about what you can/can't do.
3 Make your poster.
   Write what you can and can't do. Include when and where to meet and write your email address.

> Now turn to page 68 in the Activity Book.

COME TO

Scotland!

Scotland is a beautiful place to visit. It's got lots of amazing things to see and do.

Rivers and lakes

Scotland has got lots of rivers and lakes. You can swim in the lakes in summer but don't swim in winter – the water is very cold! You can fish in the rivers and lakes and you can sail, too.

Mountains

Scotland has got lots of high mountains. You can walk or climb there. In winter you can ski in the snow. Take warm clothes to Scotland – it's cold in the mountains!

Wildlife

You can see lots of beautiful animals and birds in Scotland. You can see eagles and deer. Take your camera to Scotland – you can take amazing photos there!

Come and visit Scotland!
Learn more at: *www.scotlandholidays.com*.

New words

climb   deer   eagle   fish(v)
lake   mountain   river   sail
ski   snow

Reading

1 (2 17) **Listen and read.**

Comprehension

2 **Read again and complete the sentences.**

Rivers and lakes

You can ¹ *swim*, ² .... and
³ ....

Mountains

You can ⁴ ...., ⁵ .... and
⁶ ....

Wildlife

You can see ⁷ .... and ⁸ ....
You can take ⁹ ....

Listening

3 (2 18) **Listen and write the numbers.**

A ☐

B ☐

C ☐

Speaking

4 **Imagine you are in another country.
Ask and answer with your partner.**

A: *Where are you?*
B: *I'm in the Republic of Ireland.*
A: *Has Ireland got lots of lakes?*
B: *No, but it's got lots of rivers.*
A: *Can you ski in Ireland?*
B: *No, you can't. Ireland hasn't got high
   mountains.*
A: *Can you see lots of animals in Ireland?*
B: *Yes, you can. Ireland has got lots of beautiful
   animals and birds.*

Project: A beautiful place in my country

5 **Find a photo of a beautiful place in
your country. Write about the place and
what you can do there.**

Hi. I'm Maria and I'm
from Argentina. Chapelco
is a beautiful place in my
country. You can walk in
the mountains and you
can see lots of amazing
animals and birds. You
can ski in the mountains
and you can swim in the
lakes. You can fish in the
rivers, too.

E Revision

1 **Write the instructions.**

| ~~Open the window!~~ Don't talk! Stop! Don't run! Close the door! Don't laugh! Sit down! Listen to me! |

1 It's hot in here.   *Open the window!*
2 That's not funny. ....
3 Here's your chair. ....
4 Listen to the teacher. ....
5 It's cold in here. ....
6 You can't go in there. ....
7 We aren't late. ....
8 I can sing. ....

2 **Choose the correct words.**

1 Let's (cook) / *draw* dinner for mum and dad.
2 You can *sing* / *act* this song with me.
3 Can we *dance* / *play* football in the park?
4 Let's *walk* / *swim* in the lake.
5 We can *make* / *cook* mum a birthday card.
6 Can you *speak* / *swim* English?
7 Let's *sing* / *play* our guitars.
8 I can *draw* / *dance* a picture of a cat.
9 Let's *listen* / *play* to our favourite music.
10 We can *ride* / *play* our new bikes.
11 He's a good actor. He can *act* / *speak* in the school play.

3 **Write sentences with *can* or *can't*.**

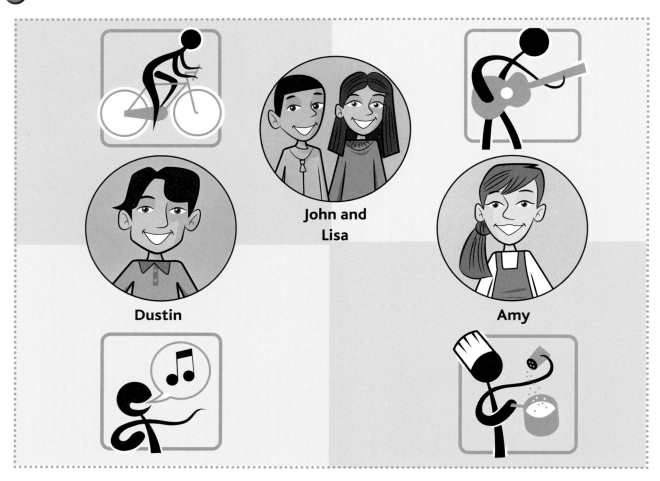

Dustin

John and Lisa

Amy

1 Dustin / ride a bike / cook
   Dustin can ride a bike but he can't cook.
2 Amy / cook / play the guitar
   ....
3 John and Lisa / sing / play the guitar
   ....

4 Dustin / play the guitar / sing
   ....
5 Amy / sing / ride a bike
   ....
6 John and Lisa / play the guitar / ride bikes
   ....

4 Look at Exercise 3. Ask and answer.

1 A: *Can Dustin cook?*
  B: *No, he can't.*
2 Can Dustin ride a bike?
3 Can John and Lisa sing?
4 Can Dustin play the guitar?
5 Can Amy cook?
6 Can John and Lisa ride bikes?

5 Game: A: Say two true sentences and one false sentence about you. B: Guess the false sentence.

A: *I can speak Spanish, I can play the piano and I can dance.*
B: *You can't speak Spanish!*
A: *Correct!*

6 Complete the dialogue with sentences a–g. There is one extra sentence.

Tom: Hey, Katie! [1] *Look at this!*
Katie: Cool! It's a school talent competition.
  [2] ....
Tom: I can sing. [3] ....
Katie: No, I can't, but I can dance.
Tom: I can dance, too. [4] ....
Katie: Good idea! We can dance to our favourite song.
Tom: OK, then. [5] ....
Katie: [6] .... I'm busy now. We can practise tomorrow.
Tom: Great!

a	What can you do?
b	Sorry, I can't.
c	~~Look at this!~~
d	Let's practise now.
e	I can't sing.
f	Let's do a dance for the competition!
g	Can you sing?

Rap: Superstar

7 🎵 2 19 Listen and complete. Then listen and rap.

Play some music, have some fun.
Music's great for everyone.
You can [1] _sing_ and play the guitar.
You can be a superstar!
Don't [2] .... now,
Don't sit down.
Wave your arms,
Dance around.
Clap your hands,
Stamp your [3] ....
[4] .... to the crazy beat!
You can be a superstar!
You can dance and sing all day.
You can hear the music [5] ....
You can jump, skip and hop
And you know you just can't [6] .... !
You can be a superstar!

Pronunciation: /æ/

8 🎵 2 20 Listen and repeat.

Sam's a **ra**pper.
That's his b**a**nd.
You c**a**n watch
And clap your h**a**nds!

My progress

9 Read and tick (✓).

I can:	
give instructions. *Walk to the door. Don't run.*	☐
talk about ability. *I can draw but I can't swim.*	☐
make suggestions. *Let's enter the competition.*	☐

> Turn to Unit 6 Check in the Activity Book on page 69.

The Fossil

Ella

Sammy

Dad

Mum

Professor Hooper

7 My name's Hooper, Professor John Hooper. I'm a scientist at the museum. Let's go to my lab!

8 At the museum ...

Now, let's look at your fossil. Hmm ... It's a very old dinosaur fish.

9 Later ...

Cool!

Thank you, Professor Hooper!

Thank you for the fossil. Here's a present for your family – tickets for the new IMAX 3D film, *The Dinosaurs of Jurassic Beach*.

THE END

New words

Be careful. dinosaur fossil plane scientist water

Reading

1 (2 21) **Listen and read.**

Comprehension

2 **Answer *True* (✓) or *False* (✗).**

1 Sammy can swim. ✓
2 Sammy's toy is a fish. ☐
3 The fossil hasn't got feet. ☐
4 Professor Hooper is a scientist. ☐
5 The fossil isn't old. ☐

3 **Match the sentences with the people.**

1 Be careful, you two. | b
2 My plane's in the water! | ☐
3 It's a fossil. | ☐
4 It's a very old dinosaur fish. | ☐
5 Look – it's got feet. | ☐

a Ella
b Mum
c Professor Hooper
d Dad
e Sammy

4 **Learn the story and act it out.**

7 My routine

A I like basketball.

Lesson aim:
- say what you like and don't like

Presentation

1 🎧 2 22 **Listen and read.**

Lily: What's on Sports Channel 1?

Asha: Let's see ... It's tennis. Do you like tennis, Lily?

Lily: No, I don't. It's boring. I like athletics and volleyball.

Robbie: I like basketball. My favourite player is Kobe Bryant.

Raj: Yeah, he's awesome. What's on Channel 2, Asha?

Asha: Football. Great!

Raj: Asha, you don't like football!

Asha: Yes, I do! This is *women's* football. It's *different*.

Robbie: Come on, Raj. Let's play table tennis in the garage.

2 🎧 2 23 **Listen and repeat the dialogue.**

English today

- What's on (Sports Channel 1)?
- It's boring.
- (He's) awesome.
- It's different.

70

Vocabulary: Sports

3 🎧 **2/24** **Listen and repeat. Then match.**

| athletics   basketball   cycling   football   hockey   karate   swimming   table tennis   tennis   volleyball |

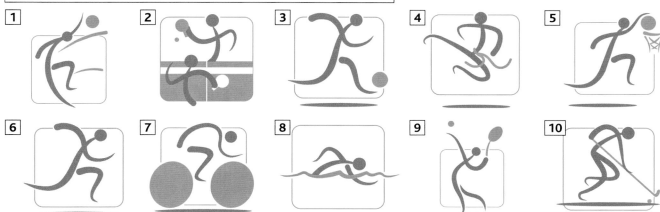

1 *volleyball*

Game

4 A: Choose a sport from Exercise 3 and mime. B: Guess the sport.

A: *What sport is this?*
B: *Is it volleyball?*
A: *Yes, it is!*

Grammar
I **like** athletics.
You **don't like** football.
Do you **like** tennis?
Yes, I **do**./No, I **don't**.

I don't like = I do not like

Speaking

5 Look at the sports in Exercise 3. Ask and answer.

A: *Do you like volleyball?*
B: *Yes, I do.*
A: *Do you like table tennis?*
B: *No, I don't.*

Writing

6 You are these people. Write sentences.

I like basketball but I don't like ...

About you

7 Write about the sports you like and don't like.

I like football and basketball but I don't like tennis. Football is my favourite sport. My favourite football team is Real Madrid and my favourite footballer is Ronaldo.

> Now turn to Unit 7A in the Activity Book. Start on page 70.

B We walk to school.

Presentation

1 🎧 2/25 **Listen and read.**

HOW WE GO
TO SCHOOL
by Lily Baker ☺

After school, we're tired. We don't walk home from school, we go by bus.

I live on Market Road. My best friends Asha and Vicky live there, too. We walk to school together. We listen to music on the way to school and we talk a lot.

My brother Robbie and his friend Raj don't walk to school. They ride their bikes. But on Fridays they have basketball practice after school. They don't go home by bike. They're tired. They go home by car with my mum.

Vocabulary: Transport

2 🎧 2/26 **Listen and repeat. Then point, ask and answer.**

| bike   boat   bus   car   motorbike   plane   taxi   train   underground (train) |

1 **A:** *Is it a bike?*
   B: *Yes, it is.*

1
2
3
4
5
6
7
8
9

Grammar

We **walk** to school.
We **don't ride** bikes to school.
They **go** to school **by** bus.
They **go** home **by** car.

Do we/they **walk** to school?
Yes, we/they **do**.
No, we/they **don't**.

Note: **by** bike/boat/bus/car/plane/taxi/train/ underground train

3 Read the text on page 72 again. Choose the correct words.

Asha, Lily and Vicky:
1 They *go / don't go* to school by bus.
2 They *go / don't go* home by bus.
3 They *walk / don't walk* home.

Raj and Robbie:
4 They *walk / ride their bikes* to school.
5 They go home *by train / by car* after basketball practice.

Speaking

4 Ask and answer about your journey to school and home.

A: *Do you go to school by bus?*
B: *No, I don't. I ride my bike. I ride my bike home, too. Do you walk to school?*
A: *Yes, I do.*
B: *Do you walk home?*
A: *No, I don't. I go home by bus.*

Listening

5 **2 27** Listen and tick (✓) how these people go to school.

1 Jake and James

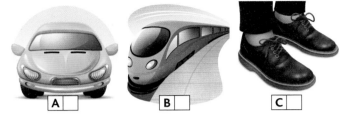

2 Rita and Ann

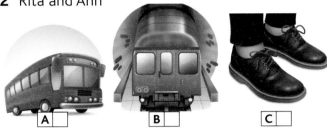

3 Laura and John

About you

6 Write about your journey to school.

How I go to school
My sister Silvia and I go to school by bus. We listen to music on the bus. After school, we don't go home by bus. We go home by car with our dad.

> Now turn to Unit 7B in the Activity Book. Start on page 74.

C What time is it?

Lesson aims:
• tell the time
• talk about routines

Presentation

 1 **Listen and read.**

Raj, Robbie and Lily are at achool.

Raj: Yum! I like chips. What time is it, Robbie?

Robbie: It's quarter to one. Why?

Raj: We have football practice at one o'clock on Wednesdays. Remember?

Robbie: Oh yeah.

Lily: It's not quarter *to* one. It's quarter *past* one.

Raj: What?

Lily: Your watch is wrong, Robbie.

Robbie: Oh, no! Now we're late for football.

Raj: Come on, Robbie. Let's run!

Lily: See you later, boys! Thanks for the chips!

2 **Listen and repeat the dialogue.**

Vocabulary: The time

3 **Listen and repeat.**

English today

• Yum!
• Remember?
• Your watch is wrong.

• See you later!
• Thanks for (the chips)!

 1
 2

one o'clock

quarter past one

 3
 4

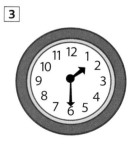

half past one

quarter to two

Grammar

What time is it?
It's quarter to (one).

Speaking

4 **Look at the clocks in Exercise 3. Ask and answer.**

1 A: *What time is it?*
B: *It's one o'clock.*

Game

5 **A: Say a time. B: Listen and draw.**

A: *It's half past two.*
B: *OK ... Is this right?*
A: *Yes! Well done!*

Listening

6 **2/31** **Listen and draw the times.**

1

2

3

4

Grammar

I **have** football practice **at** one o'clock.
You **go** home by car **every day**.
We **go** to football club **on** Wednesdays.
(= **every Wednesday**)
They **go** to football club **on** Saturdays.

Writing

7 **Look at the pictures. Write sentences.**

1 *They walk to school at half past eight every day.*

1 walk to school / every day

2 have computer club / on Mondays

3 have music club / on Wednesdays

4 play tennis / on Fridays

5 go to bed / every night

Speaking

8 **Look at the pictures in Exercise 7 and the times below. Ask and answer.**

1 **A:** *Do they walk to school at quarter past eight every day?*
  B: *No, they don't. They walk to school at half past eight every day.*

1 quarter past eight / every day
2 half past eleven / on Mondays
3 quarter past twelve / on Wednesdays
4 quarter to four / on Fridays
5 ten o'clock / every night

About you

9 **Write to a penfriend about your school week.**

My name's Marta. I live in Warsaw. I walk to school at eight o'clock every day. At half past twelve on Tuesdays I have computer club.

I like Fridays. On Fridays after school I play volleyball. I like volleyball! I go to bed at nine o'clock every night.

> Now turn to Unit 7C in the Activity Book. Start on page 78.

D Revision

1 Complete the TV guide. Use the words in the box.

athletics   basketball   cycling   football   hockey   karate
~~swimming~~   table tennis   tennis   volleyball

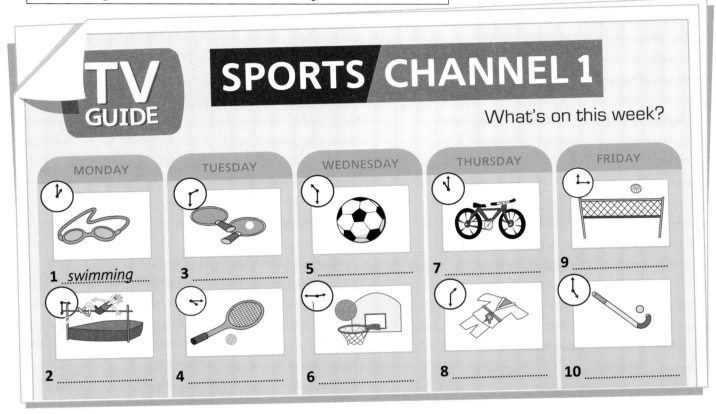

TV GUIDE

SPORTS CHANNEL 1

What's on this week?

MONDAY	TUESDAY	WEDNESDAY	THURSDAY	FRIDAY
1 _swimming_	3	5	7	9 ....
2	4	6	8	10 ....

2 Look at the TV guide in Exercise 1. Ask and answer.

1 A: *What's on Monday at one o'clock?*
B: *Swimming.*

1 Monday / one o'clock
2 Tuesday / quarter past four

3 Wednesday / half past ten
4 Thursday / half past one
5 Friday / quarter past twelve

3 Complete the crossword.

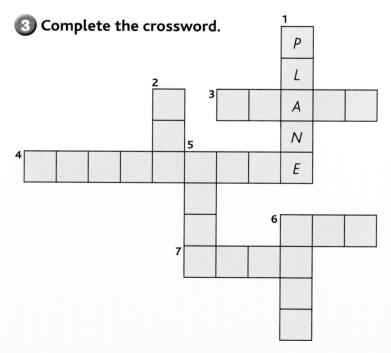

1 P
L
A
3
N
E
2
5
4
6
7

Across

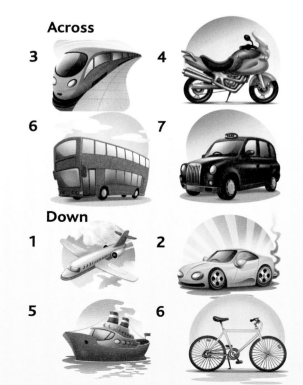

3
4
6
7

Down

1
2
5
6

4 Do you like these sports? Look and tick (✓) or cross (x). Then ask and answer to complete the table for your partner.

Do you like basketball?

Yes, I do./No, I don't.

	Me	My partner
Basketball		
Athletics		
Swimming		
Cycling		

5 Complete the email with the correct forms of the verbs.

---

send   save

Subject: Hello!

Dear Lisa,

My name's Helen. I ¹ *live* (live) in London with my family. We ² .... (not/live) near my school. I ³ .... (not/walk) to school. I ⁴ .... (go) to school by bus. My brothers ⁵ .... (not/go) to my school. They ⁶ .... (ride) their bikes to their school every day. I ⁷ .... (have) Art club on Mondays but my brothers ⁸ .... (not/have) Art club. They ⁹ .... (go) to tennis club. ¹⁰ .... (you/live) near your school? ¹¹ .... (you/cycle) to school? Write soon!

Love,

Helen

Song: I love sports

6 🎵 2/32 Listen and complete. Then listen and sing.

I love sports — they're lots of fun.
I think they're really cool.
On Mondays there's ¹ *karate* club
And ² .... after school.

On Wednesdays I have volleyball
With friends at half past two.
On Fridays I have ³ ....
And I do ⁴ ...., too.

On Saturdays and Sundays
I cycle with my friend.
We ⁵ .... to our sports club
And we have fun all weekend!

Pronunciation: /ɪ/

7 2/33 Listen and repeat.

Fish and chips is an English dish.
Tim likes chips and his cat likes fish!

My progress

8 Read and tick (✓).

I can:	
say what I like and don't like. *I like basketball but I don't like football.*	☐
talk about my journey to school. *We walk to school.* *We go by bus.*	☐
tell the time. *It's quarter to one.* *It's half past four.*	☐
talk about routines. *We go to football club on Wednesdays.*	☐

> Turn to Unit 7 Check in the Activity Book on page 82.

Fun Time!

Look at the photos and write the sports. Then find the name of the sports star.

◯ [¹O] ◯ ◯ [²☐] ◯ ◯ ◯

◯ ◯ ◯ ◯ ◯ [⁷☐] ◯

◯ ◯ ◯ ◯ [³☐] ◯ [⁴☐] [⁵☐] ◯ ◯

The sports star is
K ^{1}O____ ^{2}____ ^{3}____
^{4}____ R Y ^{5}____ ^{6}____ ^{7}____.

◯ ◯ [⁶☐] ◯ ◯ ◯

JUST JOKING!

How can you get four elephants into a sports car?

Two in the front and two in the back!

Make a spinner. Then play the game in pairs or groups.

START

1 What's your name?

2 What day is it today?

3 How old are you?

4 What's this?

5 What's your address?

11 What's your favourite animal?

10 What colour is this?

9 SPIN AGAIN

8 Do you like football?

7 Where are you from?

6 What's your phone number?

12 Are you happy today?

13 Have you got a pet?

14 Name five things in your bedroom.

15 What's this?

16 What kind of hair have you got?

17 Can you ride a horse?

23 Who's your favourite sports star?

22 SPIN AGAIN

21 What's this?

20 Name five things in your school bag.

19 Is it Saturday today?

18 MISS A TURN

24 Have you got a brother?

25 What colour is your pencil case?

26 What colour eyes have you got?

27 What's this?

28 Can you sing?

29 Do you like swimming?

FINISH

34 What sport can you play with this?

33 MISS A TURN

32 What time is it?

31 What's your favourite sport?

30 Can your dad play the guitar?

8 Work and play

A He works at night.

Presentation

1 (2/34) **Listen and read.**

Mr Patel: Hello, you two! Right, it's time for my cornflakes.

Robbie: That's funny. Does your dad have cornflakes for dinner?

Raj: No, he doesn't. He has cornflakes for breakfast.

Robbie: But it's six o'clock in the evening!

Raj: I know. He's a pilot and he works at night.

Robbie: Really? When does he sleep?

Raj: During the day. He comes home at seven o'clock in the morning, goes to bed and sleeps all day.

Robbie: You're kidding! I want to be a pilot!

2 (2/35) **Listen and repeat the dialogue.**

English today

· That's funny.
· You're kidding!

80

Vocabulary: Routines

3 (2/36) **Listen and repeat. Then mime the routines.**

> get dressed   get up   go to bed
> go to school   have breakfast
> have dinner   have lunch   wake up

4 **Put the routines in Exercise 3 in the order you do them. Then write five sentences about you.**

I wake up at seven o'clock.

Grammar

He **works** at night.
She **doesn't work** during the day.
Does he/she work at night?
Yes, he **does**.
No, she **doesn't**.
What time/When does she wake up?
She wakes up at seven o'clock.

5 **Look at the dialogue in Exercise 1 again. Complete the sentences about Mr Patel.**

Mr Patel

1 Mr Patel _has_ cornflakes for breakfast.
2 He .... cornflakes for dinner.
3 He .... at night.
4 He .... home at seven o'clock.
5 He .... all day.

Listening

6 (2/37) **What time does Lazy Linda do these things? Listen and match.**

> 1.30   6.00   ~~10.00~~   10.45
> 11.15   12.30

1 wake up _10.00_
2 get up ....
3 have breakfast ....
4 have lunch ....
5 have dinner ....
6 go to bed ....

Speaking

7 **Ask your partner questions about Lazy Linda.**

A: *What time/When does she wake up?*
B: *She wakes up at ten o'clock.*

About you

8 **Choose your favourite sportsperson. Write about his/her day.**

RAFAEL'S BUSY ROUTINE

This is Rafael Nadal. He's a Spanish tennis player. He gets up at six o'clock every day. He has breakfast at half past six. He gets dressed and has tennis practice in the morning. He has lunch and plays tennis again in the afternoon. He has dinner at eight o'clock. He doesn't play tennis in the evening. He goes to bed at ten o'clock. His day is very busy!

> Now turn to Unit 8A in the Activity Book. Start on page 83.

B Can we have our picnic?

Lesson aim:
• ask permission

Presentation

1 **Listen and read.**

Robbie and Lily are with their mum in London.

Robbie: I'm hungry. Can we have our picnic now, please, Mum?

Mum: No, you can't. Sorry. It's only eleven o'clock.

Robbie: OK, but can I have a packet of crisps?

Mum: All right. Yes, you can.

Lily: Can I take a photo of Buckingham Palace, Mum?

Mum: Yes, sure.

Robbie: Can I be in your photo, too, Lily?

Lily: No, you can't, Robbie. Move! You're in the way!

2 **Listen and repeat the dialogue.**

English today

• Move!
• You're in the way!

Vocabulary: Snack food

3 **Listen and repeat. Then point, ask and answer.**

| banana   bar of chocolate   biscuit   burger   hot dog |
| packet of crisps   sandwich   yoghurt |

1 A: *Is it a banana?*
   B: *No, it isn't. It's a burger.*

82

4 Complete the puzzle and find the mystery word.

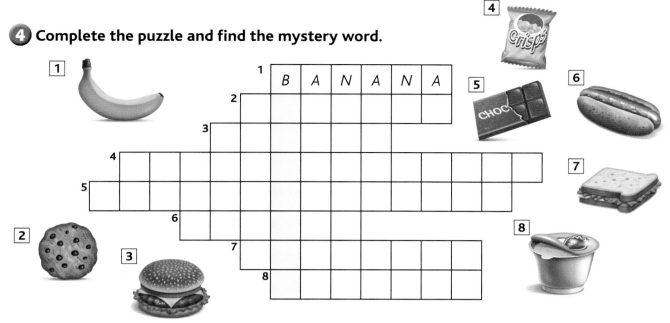

| | | B | A | N | A | N | A |
| | | | | | | | |

The mystery word is: ....

Grammar

Can I have a packet of crisps?
Yes, you **can**./Yes, sure.
Can we have our picnic now, please?
No, you **can't**. Sorry.

can't = cannot

Speaking

5 Ask and answer with your partner. You can only have healthy food!

- apple (✓)
- banana (✓)
- ice cream (✗)
- yoghurt (✓)
- burger (✗)
- hot dog (✗)
- bar of chocolate (✗)

- biscuit (✗)
- sandwich (✓)
- cake (✗)
- packet of crisps (✗)

A: *Can I have an apple, please?*
B: *Yes, you can.*
A: *Can I have a bar of chocolate, please?*
B: *No, you can't. Sorry.*

6 Write the questions for the situations. Use the pictures to help you.

1 You're hungry.
   Can I have an apple, please?
2 You're bored.

   ....
3 You're tired.

   ....
4 You're hot.

   ....
5 You're cold.

   ....

Writing

7 Write a text message to your mum, dad or family member.

Hi Mum. Can Piotr and Marek come to our house this evening, please? Can we watch a film and can we have hot dogs and burgers? Thanks! Artur :-)

> Now turn to Unit 8B in the Activity Book. Start on page 87.

Communication

Speaking: Buy food and drink

1   **Listen and read.**

Robbie and Lily are at the park.

1

Man:	Hi! Can I help you?
Robbie:	Yes, can I have a strawberry ice cream, please?
Man:	Yes, certainly. Here you are. Anything else?
Robbie:	No, thanks.

2

Lily:	Excuse me. How much are the bananas?
Man:	They're 70p each.
Lily:	And how much is a cola?
Man:	It's £1.
Lily:	OK. Can I have a banana and a cola, please?

3

Man:	Sure. Here you are.
Robbie:	How much is that altogether?
Man:	£3.20.
Robbie:	Here's £5.
Man:	Thank you. Here's your change. Have a nice day!

British money

Pounds

£1 = one pound   £5 = five pounds

£2.50 = two pounds fifty

Pence

10p = ten pence (p)   50p = fifty pence (p)

English today

Buy food and drink
- Can I help you?
- Can I have a/an ..., please?
- Here you are.

- Anything else?
- How much is/are ... ?
- How much is that altogether?
- Here's your change.

2 **Write the prices.**

1 £1.10
  one pound ten

2 £5.25
  ....

3 30p
  ....

4 £6.50
  ....

5 45p
  ....

6 £3.40
  ....

3 **2 42** **Choose the correct words. Then listen and check.**

Man: Hi! Can I ¹(help)/ change you?

Asha: Yes. ² *Here / Can* I have a chocolate ice cream, please?

Man: Yes, certainly. ³ *Here / How* you are. Anything else?

Asha: No, thanks.

Raj: Excuse me. How ⁴ *much / many* are the apples?

Man: They're fifty ⁵ *pounds / pence* each.

Raj: And how much is a chicken sandwich?

Man: It's £2.50.

Raj: OK. Can I have an apple and a chicken sandwich, ⁶ *please / thank you*?

Man: Sure. Here you are.

Asha: How much is that altogether?

Man: That's four ⁷ *pounds / pence* seventy.

Asha: Here's £5.

Man: Thank you. Here's your ⁸ *pounds / change*.

Writing: Design a menu

5 **Ask and answer with your partner.**

1 **A:** *How much are the apples?*
  B: *They're fifty pence.*

1 apples
2 crisps
3 burgers
4 bars of chocolate
5 sandwiches
6 ice creams

6 **Look at the menu and write the prices. Then say.**

1 *A sandwich and two packets of crisps is three pounds fifty.*

1 a sandwich and two packets of crisps = __£3.50__
2 a burger and an apple = ...
3 two cakes and an apple = ...
4 two sandwiches and a bar of chocolate = ...
5 two burgers and a packet of biscuits = ...
6 a packet of crisps and two bananas = ...

Your turn

4 **Use the phrases in English today to write a dialogue.**

Student A: You work in the school shop. Sandwiches are £1.50 (one pound fifty), bars of chocolate are 60p (sixty pence), biscuits are 40p (forty pence) and drinks are 50p (fifty pence).

Student B: You want to buy a sandwich and a bar of chocolate or a biscuit. You've got £2 (two pounds).

A: *Hi! Can I help you?*
B: *Yes. Can I have ....*

MR. SNACKMAN'S
SNACKS

Burgers	£3.00
Sandwiches (cheese/chicken)	£2.50
Packet of crisps	50p
Ice creams	£1.70
Cola	£1.00
Bars of chocolate	50p
Packet of biscuits	50p
Cakes	65p
Apples/Bananas	50p

Your turn

7 **Make a menu for your school snack shop.**

1 Choose your favourite snacks.
2 Decide the price of each snack.
3 Write and design your menu. Write the prices in British money.

> Now turn to page 91 in the Activity Book.

BUSY WEEKENDS!

Top five free time activities for teenagers

IN THE UK 🇬🇧	IN THE USA 🇺🇸
1 watch TV	1 meet or talk to friends
2 meet friends	2 watch TV
3 chat online	3 play computer games
4 play sports with friends	4 listen to music
5 read books and magazines	5 play sports in a team

Jared, 10

Becky, 11

Jared is American and he lives in the USA. His cousin Becky is British and she lives in the UK. They both have busy weekends.

I'm Jared and I live in Tampa, Florida in the USA. I like weekends. On Saturdays I get up at eight o'clock — I have basketball practice at nine o'clock. After practice, I have lunch with my family. We go to Pizza King. It's my favourite pizza restaurant. On Sundays I play in a baseball team in the morning. In the afternoon I meet my friends but we don't play baseball — we play computer games! I have a great new game called Rock Band 6. I don't have school on Sundays so I go to bed at ten o'clock on Saturdays.

My cousin Becky lives in Brighton in the UK. She's lazy! She gets up at ten o'clock on Saturdays and watches TV with her sister. In the afternoon she has lunch with her best friend Lucy. On Saturday evenings they go to a disco at the youth club. On Sunday mornings she goes shopping with her mum. In the evening she chats with me online. I like Becky. She's cool.

New words

baseball   chat   computer games
disco   meet   shopping

Reading

1 **2/43** **Listen and read.**

Comprehension

2 **Read again and tick (✓) or cross (✗).**

	Jared	Becky
Have basketball practice	✓	✗
Chat online		
Go to a disco		
Play baseball		

3 **Look at the activities in the table in Exercise 2. Ask and answer about Jared and Becky.**

A: *Does Jared have basketball practice?*
B: *Yes, he does.*

4 **Complete the table with your top five activities.**

MY TOP FIVE FREE TIME ACTIVITIES

1 ....

2 ....

3 ....

4 ....

5 ....

Listening

5 **2/44** **Listen and tick (✓) the correct activity for each person.**

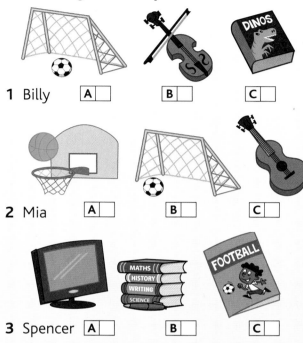

1 Billy   A ☐   B ☐   C ☐

2 Mia   A ☐   B ☐   C ☐

3 Spencer   A ☐   B ☐   C ☐

Speaking

6 **Talk about your typical weekend. Ask and answer.**

1   A: *What time do you get up on Saturdays?*
    B: *I get up at nine o'clock. What time ...?*

1   What time do you get up on Saturdays?
2   When do you have breakfast?
3   What do you do in the afternoon?
4   Do you play sport on Sundays?

Project: My weekend

7 **Write about your weekend.**

MY WEEKEND

Hi, I'm Alessandra and I'm from Palermo in Italy. This is my weekend. I get up at ten o'clock on Saturdays and Sundays. I watch TV and read magazines on Saturday mornings. On Sundays we...

E Revision

1 Unscramble the words.

1 keaw pu _wake up_

2 teg pu ....

3 tge sedsdre ....

4 veha arkebtafs ....

5 og ot clohos ....

6 ahev cuhln ....

7 ahev nrenid ....

8 og ot deb ....

2 Use the words in Exercise 1 to write sentences about your day.

I wake up at seven o'clock.

3 Look at the picture. Find and circle seven foods.

4 Look at the foods in Exercise 3. Ask and answer.

A: *Do you like bananas?*
B: *Yes, I do./No, I don't.*

5 Write the correct forms of the verbs.

TOM'S WEEK

Tom is my friend. He
¹ _wakes_ (wake)
up at seven o'clock.
He ² .... (have) breakfast at
half past seven and he
³ .... (go) to school at eight
o'clock. But on Saturdays he
⁴ .... (not/go) to school. He
⁵ .... (do) his homework. Then
he ⁶ .... (play) football. He
⁷ .... (not/watch) TV on
Saturday evenings. He ⁸ ....
(go) to a disco. ⁹ .... (he/have)
fun? Yes, he ¹⁰ .... (do)!

6 Write about Tom's and your week.

Tom wakes up at seven o'clock but I wake up at half past eight.

7 Write short dialogues. Act them out.

1 A: *Can I have a packet of crisps, please?*
B: *No, you can't. Sorry.*

1	have / packet of crisps	✗
2	take / a photo	✓
3	play / on the computer	✓
4	go / to the disco	✗
5	wear / your jacket	✗
6	watch / the baseball game	✓

8 Complete the dialogue with sentences a–g. Then act it out.

Woman: ¹ *Hi! Can I help you?*
Lily: Yes, can I have a bar of chocolate, please?
Woman: ² ....
Lily: No, thanks.
Robbie: Excuse me. How much are the apples?
Woman: ³ ....
Robbie: And how much is a sandwich?
Woman: ⁴ ....
Robbie: OK. Can I have an apple and a cheese sandwich, please?
Woman: ⁵ ....
Lily: How much is that altogether?
Woman: ⁶ ....
Lily: Here's £5.
Woman: ⁷ ....

a	That's £2.30.
b	Sure. Here you are.
c	It's £1.50.
d	Yes, certainly. Anything else?
e	They're 30p each.
f	~~Hi! Can I help you?~~
g	Thank you. Here's your change. Have a nice day!

Rap: Tasty treats

9 🔊 ²⁄₄₅ Listen and complete. Then listen and rap.

Can I have a ¹ _sandwich_ , please?
I like chicken, I like cheese.
Chocolate, biscuits,
² ...., too.
Tasty treats for me and you.
We can buy nice food at
³ ....
Our school shop is really cool.

You can ⁴ ....
a tasty treat.
Lots of lovely things to eat!
How much ⁵ .... have you got?
It's OK, I've got a lot!
I can buy a snack for you.
Let's buy ⁶ .... and colas, too.

Pronunciation: /tʃ/

10 🔊 ²⁄₄₆ Listen and repeat.

What's for lun**ch**? Sandwi**ch**es, please!
One with **ch**icken, one with **ch**eese.
Tasty **ch**ips and **ch**ocolate, too.
Lots of lun**ch** for me and you!

My progress

11 Read and tick (✓).

I can:	
talk about routines. *He gets up at six o'clock.*	☐
ask permission. *Can I take a photo, please?*	☐
buy food and drink. A: *Can I have a strawberry ice cream, please?* B: *Here you are.*	☐

> Turn to Unit 8 Check in the Activity Book on page 92.

BANANA BOY

Chris

On Saturday Chris and his friends go to the park ...

Adam   Lisa   Banana Boy

New words

safe   save the day
secret   Yum!

Reading

1 🎧 2 47 **Listen and read.**

Comprehension

2 **Put the story in the correct order.**

a Lisa buys an ice cream. *1*
b The children wait for the bus. ....
c Lisa sees Banana Boy's face. ....
d Banana Boy saves Adam. ....
e Banana Boy saves Lisa's ice cream. ....
f The children watch a baseball game. ....
g Banana Boy saves Lisa. ....

3 **Learn the story and act it out.**

Word list

Unit 1

Lesson A
The alphabet

Lesson B
Family members:
father
dad
mother
mum
brother
sister
uncle
aunt
cousin
grandfather
grandad
grandmother
grandma

Lesson C
Days of the week:
Monday
Tuesday
Wednesday
Thursday
Friday
Saturday
Sunday

Numbers 0–50

Unit 2

Lesson A
Possessions (1):
apple
bike
book
camera
computer
football
ice cream
skateboard
TV
umbrella

Colours:
black
blue
brown
green
grey
orange
pink
purple
red
white
yellow

Lesson B
Everyday objects:
bag
comic
dictionary
eraser
jacket
mobile phone
notebook
pen
pencil case
ruler

Unit 3

Lesson A
Feelings:
cold
happy
hot
hungry
ill
sad
thirsty
tired

Lesson B
Countries:
Argentina
Australia
India
Italy
Poland
Spain
the UK
the USA

Lesson C
Wild animals:
crocodile
elephant
giraffe
lion
monkey
ostrich
parrot
polar bear
snake
zebra

Unit 4

Lesson A
Clothes:
dress
hat
jacket
jeans
jumper
shoe(s)
skirt
trainer(s)
trousers
T-shirt

Lesson B
Rooms and furniture:
bathroom
bedroom
kitchen
living room
bath
bed
chair
cooker
cupboard
fridge
sofa
table

Unit 5

Lesson A

Possessions (2):

a CD player
an MP3 player
a pair of sunglasses
a sleeping bag
a tent
a torch
a watch

Lesson B

Appearance:

black
blonde
brown
red
long
medium-length
short
blue
brown
green
grey

Lesson C

Pets:

bird
cat
dog
fish
hamster
lizard
rabbit
tortoise

Parts of animals:

body
ear
feet
foot
head
leg
nose
paw
tail
wing

Unit 6

Lesson A

Action verbs:

Close the door!
Don't eat here!
Don't laugh!
Don't run!
Don't talk!
Listen to me!
Open the window!
Sit down!
Stand up!
Stop!

Lesson B

Activity verbs:

act
cook
dance
draw
make a cake
play football
play the guitar
ride a bike
sing
speak Spanish
swim

Unit 7

Lesson A

Sports:

athletics
basketball
cycling
football
hockey
karate
swimming
table tennis
tennis
volleyball

Lesson B

Transport:

bike
boat
bus
car
motorbike
plane
taxi
train
underground (train)

Lesson C

The time:

(one) o'clock
quarter past (one)
half past (one)
quarter to (two)

Unit 8

Lesson A

Routines:

get dressed
get up
go to bed
go to school
have breakfast
have dinner
have lunch
wake up

Lesson B

Snack food:

banana
bar of chocolate
biscuit
burger
hot dog
packet of crisps
sandwich
yoghurt

Lenny's grammar lessons

1 Subject pronouns

I	I'm Lenny.
you	You're nice.
he	He's Robbie.
she	She's Lily.
it	It's a house.
we	We're happy.
you	You're friends.
they	They're Raj and Asha.

2 Verb: *to be* positive

Long	Short
I am Lenny.	I'm Lenny.
You are ten.	You're ten.
He is Robbie.	He's Robbie.
She is Lily.	She's Lily.
It is a dog.	It's a dog.
We are friends.	We're friends.
You are sisters.	You're sisters.
They are Raj and Asha.	They're Raj and Asha.

3 Verb: *to be* negative and questions

Negative

Long	Short
I am not ten.	I'm not ten.
You are not eight.	You aren't eight.
He is not happy.	He isn't happy.
She is not hungry.	She isn't hungry.
It is not cold.	It isn't cold.
We are not teachers.	We aren't teachers.
You are not brothers.	You aren't brothers.
They are not tired.	They aren't tired.

Questions and short answers

Am I funny?	Yes, you are./No, you aren't.
Are you eleven?	Yes, I am./No, I'm not.
Is he a student?	Yes, he is./No, he isn't.
Is she ten?	Yes, she is./No, she isn't.
Is it a dog?	Yes, it is./No, it isn't.
Are we friends?	Yes, we are./No, we aren't.
Are you sisters?	Yes, we are./No, we aren't.
Are they happy?	Yes, they are./No, they aren't.

4 Questions

What's your name?
My name's Lenny.

How old are you?
I'm ten.

Who's he?
He's Lenny.

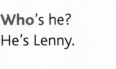

What day is it today?
It's Wednesday.

Where are you from?
I'm from the UK.

5 Possessive adjectives

my	**My** name is Lenny.
your	**Your** name is Alex.
his	**His** name is Robbie.
her	**Her** name is Lily.
its	**Its** name is Spot.
our	**Our** names are Alex and Robbie.
your	**Your** names are Robbie and Lily.
their	**Their** names are Raj and Asha.

6 Possessive 's

She's Lenny**'s** mum.

7 Noun plurals

One		Two or more
one lion	⟶	two lion**s**
one snake	⟶	two snake**s**
one ostrich	⟶	two ostrich**es**

8 Indefinite article: *a*/*an*

It's **a**	**b**ook/**c**at/**p**en.
It's **an**	**a**pple/**i**ce cream/**u**mbrella.
What colour is it?	It's red.

9 | Definite article: *the*

Where's **the** cooker?   It's in **the** kitchen.
Where's **the** cat?   It's on **the** chair.

10 | *This*, *that* and *these*

What's **this**?   It's a bike.
What's **that**?   It's a ball.

This is an apple.
These are ice creams.

11

Prepositions of place

Where's the cat?

It's **in** the box.

It's **on** the box.

It's **under** the box.

Verb: *have got*

Positive

Long

I **have got** long hair.
You **have got** blue eyes.
He **has got** a brother.
She **has got** a sister.
It **has got** a ball.

We **have got** short hair.
You **have got** brown eyes.
They **have got** black hair.

Short

I've **got** long hair.
You've **got** blue eyes.
He's **got** a brother.
She's **got** a sister.
It's **got** a ball.

We've **got** short hair.
You've **got** brown eyes.
They've **got** black hair.

Negative

Long

I **have not got** red hair.
You **have not got** short hair.
He **has not got** a computer.
She **has not got** a bike.
It **has not got** short ears.
We **have not got** blue eyes.
You **have not got** green eyes.
They **have not got** long hair.

Short

I **haven't got** red hair.
You **haven't got** short hair.
He **hasn't got** a computer.
She **hasn't got** a bike.
It **hasn't got** short ears.
We **haven't got** blue eyes.
You **haven't got** green eyes.
They **haven't got** long hair.

Questions and short answers

Have I **got** short hair?
Have you **got** green eyes?
Has he **got** a sister?
Has she **got** a brother?
Has it **got** long ears?
Have we **got** brown eyes?
Have you **got** blue eyes?
Have they **got** long hair?

Yes, you **have**./No, you **haven't**.
Yes, I **have**./No, I **haven't**.
Yes, he **has**./No, he **hasn't**.
Yes, she **has**./No, she **hasn't**.
Yes, it **has**./No, it **hasn't**.
Yes, you **have**./No, you **haven't**.
Yes, we **have**./No, we **haven't**.
Yes, they **have**./No, they **haven't**.

What kind of hair **have** you **got**?
I've **got** short grey hair.

13 Verb: *can*

Positive

I **can** sing.
You **can** ride a bike.
He **can** jump.
She **can** run.
It **can** talk.
We **can** play football.
You **can** swim.
They **can** fly.

Negative

I **can't** play football.
You **can't** run.
He **can't** swim.
She **can't** ride a bike.
It **can't** fly.
We **can't** jump.
You **can't** sing.
They **can't** talk.

Questions and short answers

Can I play the guitar?
Can you run?
Can he play basketball?
Can she dance?
Can it jump?
Can we sing?
Can you write?
Can they walk?

Yes, you **can**./No, you **can't**.
Yes, I **can**./No, I **can't**.
Yes, he **can**./No, he **can't**.
Yes, she **can**./No, she **can't**.
Yes, it **can**./No, it **can't**.
Yes, you **can**./No, you **can't**.
Yes, we **can**./No, we **can't**.
Yes, they **can**./No, they **can't**.

Can I have an apple, please?
No, you **can't**. Sorry.
Can I have a banana, please?
Yes, you **can**.

14 Imperatives

Positive

Stand up!
Open the window!
Sit down!
Close the door!

Negative

Don't stand up!
Don't open the window!
Don't sit down!
Don't close the door!

15   Present simple

Positive

I **like** apples.
You **like** oranges.
He **likes** football.
She **likes** basketball.
It **likes** fish.
We **like** music.
You **like** English.
They **like** sport.

Negative

I **don't like** oranges.
You **don't like** apples.
He **doesn't like** basketball.
She **doesn't like** football.
It **doesn't like** ice cream.
We **don't like** sport.
You **don't like** fish.
They **don't like** music.

Questions and short answers

Do I **play** football on Mondays?	Yes, you **do**./No, you **don't**.
Do you **have** guitar lessons?	Yes, I **do**./No, I **don't**.
Does he **live** in a big house?	Yes, he **does**./No, he **doesn't**.
Does she **like** music?	Yes, she **does**./No, she **doesn't**.
Does it **play** in the garden?	Yes, it **does**./No, it **doesn't**.
Do we **watch** TV?	Yes, you **do**./No, you **don't**.
Do you **live** in London?	Yes, we **do**./No, we **don't**.
Do they **like** apples?	Yes, they **do**./No, they **don't**.

16   Prepositions of time

I have lunch **at** one o'clock.
We go to school **every day**.
He plays football **on** Fridays. (= every Friday)

Pearson Education Limited
Edinburgh Gate
Harlow
Essex CM20 2JE
England
and Associated Companies throughout the world.

www.pearsonelt.com

© Pearson Education Limited 2013

The right of Tamzin Thompson and David Todd to be identified as authors of this Work has been asserted by them in accordance with the Copyright, Designs and Patents Act 1988.

First published 2013
Eight impression 2019

ISBN: 978-1-4479-0105-1

Set in Bliss Light 12.5/16pt
Printed in Italy by L.E.G.O. S.p.A.

Acknowledgements
The publishers and authors would like to thank the following people for their feedback and comments during the development of the material:
Argentina: Alicia Artusi and Cristina Djivanian
Poland: Beata Bużan, Agnieszka Gil, Małgorzata Kuc and Katarzyna Szwejkowska

Picture Credits
The publisher would like to thank the following for their kind permission to reproduce their photographs:

(Key: b-bottom; c-centre; l-left; r-right; t-top)

Alamy Images: acestock 43tr, Aflo FotoAgency 70 (TV screen), Asia Images Group Pte Ltd 28t (inset), Ben Molyneux People 44 (Jenny), blickwinkel 64b, Colin Underhill 72tc, Cultura Creative 53cl, dbimages 51br, Enigma 78tr, Image Source 88br, Joe Fox 42tc, Justin Kase zsixz 78tl, mainpicture 78bl, Mike Goldwater 72c, Oote Boe Photography 42bc, PhotosIndia.com LLC 33tl, RTimages 17 (1), Tetra Images 86bl; **Corbis:** BPI / Marc Atkins 5bl, Chris Brunskill / BPI 29tl, John A. Angelillo 5br, Larry Williams 21cr, Lucy Nicholson 78cr, Rick Gomez 9br, Shannon Fagan 49 (Simon), Waller McBride 7br; **Egmont UK Ltd London:** From War Horse by Michael Morpurgo. Copyright 1982 Michael Morpurgo. Cover illustration copyright 2006 National Theatre from the poster for the National Theatre's stage adaptation of War Horse, first staged October 2007. Published by Egmont UK Ltd London and used with permission 20c; **Fotolia.com:** 12_tribes 20cr, 12742219 49 (2), 49 (6), ANP 34 (6), Anthony Rosenberg 44 (3), bkhphoto 49 (1), 49 (9), BlessEdd 49 (8), borabajk 41bc, c 84cl, 84b, Calek 20br, Christian Delbert 41tc, Colette 34 (3), Connie Wade 41 (3), Eric Isselee 41 (1), Gail Johnson 64c, gallas 34bl, Gino Santa Maria 31tr, graham tomlin 49 (4), Gudmund 64t, kertis 41 (2), kmit 17 (3), Marlee 49 (3), 49 (7), Michelle Lemon 10cl, Monkey Business 6 (Jake), Mytho 30tr, Oleksandr Moroz 49 (5), Pat Lalli 30cl, Patryssia 43br, picsfive 17 (5), robootb 17 (2), Rohit Seth 7 (Devina), rufar 17 (4), Sujit Mahapatra 84cr, Taalvi 34 (4), Werg 53br, Yuri Arcurs 6 (Janice); **Getty Images:** Martin Harvey 30tl; iStockphoto: alle12 44 (2), Ana Abejon 49 (Nikki), Anthony Rosenberg 44 (4), Vikram Raghuvanshi 49 (Sunita); **Pearson Education Ltd:** Jon Barlow 4, 6 (Alex), 6 (Eric), 6 (Jerry), 6 (Lily), 6 (Robbie), 6 (Sally), 6t, 7 (Asha), 7 (Deepa), 7 (Raj), 7 (Sanjay), 8, 14, 16t, 18t, 23cl, 26, 28t, 30cr, 31tl, 31tc, 31cl, 31cr, 36, 38t, 40t, 40b, 42cr, 43bl, 44 (Tom), 48, 50t, 51tl, 51tr, 51c, 51cl, 51cr, 52t, 58, 60, 61t, 61tc, 61b, 61bc, 62, 70, 72tl, 74t, 80, 81bl, 82t, 84t, 89l; Pearson Education Ltd: BananaStock 6 (Patricia), 6 (Peter), Coleman Yuen. Pearson Education Asia Ltd 44 (Lin), Creatas 34bc, Image Source 33cl (flag), 33bl (flag), Photodisc. Siede Preis Photography 34 (5), Sophie Bluy. Pearson Education Ltd 20 (3), Studio 8. Pearson Education Ltd 20tc; **Photofusion Picture Library:** Digital Nation 72tr; Press Association Images: Alik Keplicz 57b, Ron Edmonds / AP 13bl, Sang Tan / AP

5cr, Teds. Warren / AP 29br; **Rex Features:** Aflo 81r, Broadimage 29bc, 35tl, Broadimage 29bc, 35tl, Greg Allen 5cl, keystoneUSA-ZUMA 7tr, Picture Perfect 29bl, Tim Rooke 29tc; **Robert Harding World Imagery:** marka 65r; **Shutterstock.com:** auremar 67cr, Chamille White 41c, cynoclub 53bl, Dudarev Mikhail 65tl, Gelpi 33bl, Gerrit_de_Vries 34 (2), Goodluz 44 (Lisa), Gulei Ivan 44 (1), iofoto 67cl, karkas 17 (6), Lorraine Swanson 34br, Maxim Kulko 17 (8), Monkey Business Images 20 (2), 77bl, Monkey Business Images 20 (2), 77bl, Nataliia Melnychuk 53tl, Phase 4 Photography 42cl, Poznukhov Yuriy 65bl, r.nagy 42c, Sandra Van Der Steen 33cl, Tungphoto 17 (7), V.S. anandhakrishna 42bl, 43cl, Volodymyr Krasyuk 34 (1), YlinPhoto 65cl; **starfishLA:** Micah Smith 13cl; **SuperStock:** age fotostock 86cl, Corbis 78cl; **The Kobal Collection:** Marvel / Paramount 19bl, Warner Bros / DCcomics 19cl

Cover images: *Front:* **Pearson Education Ltd:** Jon Barlow

All other images © Pearson Education

Our special thanks to the following for their help during location photography:

Amherst School, Battersea Dogs Home, KGLC Camping, Paradise Wildlife Park, The Royal Parks.

Illustrated by Ilias Arahovitis (9, 30, 31, 32, 39, 46, 49, 54, 56, 68, 69, 71, 72, 73, 76, 83, 96), Kathy Baxendale (10, 15, 20, 31, 37, 42) Paco Cavero (11, 23, 24, 25, 32, 33, 37, 45, 49, 55, 57, 60, 67, 75, 77, 89, 90, 91), Andrew Hennessey (18, 22, 27, 33, 44, 50, 53, 59, 66, 71), James Horvath (12, 35, 38, 39, 44, 74, 75, 76, 79, 82, 87), Chris Simpson (11, 12, 13, 15, 23, 33, 35, 45, 52, 55, 56, 67, 77, 78, 89), Simon Smith (12, 15, 17, 21, 22, 27, 37, 45, 54, 55, 66, 73, 88, 95, 96), Gary Swift (3, 5, 6, 9, 15, 17, 27, 29, 31, 37, 49, 59, 61, 71, 73, 74, 79, 81).

La presente publicación se ajusta la cartografía oficial establecida por el Poder Ejecutivo Nacional Argentino a través del IGN – Ley 22.963 – y fue aprobada por el Expte. N° GG13 1696/5